Starter

WORKBOOK

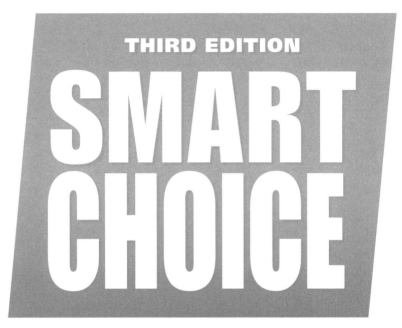

THIRD EDITION

SMART CHOICE

SMART LEARNING
on the page and *on the move*

Ken Wilson / Thomas Healy

OXFORD
UNIVERSITY PRESS

CONTENTS

UNITS

1 | I'm a student.

VOCABULARY

1 Look at the pictures. Write the words in the crossword puzzle.

Across

1.

3.

Down

2.

4.

5.

7.

6.

2 Write the missing letters.

1. a _c_ t _o_ r

2. w ___ ___   ___ e ___ i ___ ___ e r

3. b ___ ___ i ___ e ___ s w ___ ___ a n

4. ___ h e ___

5. ___ ___ u ___ e n ___

6. w ___ ___ t ___ r

LANGUAGE PRACTICE

1 Complete the sentences. Use *am*, *are*, or *is*.

1. Angela _is_____ from Tokyo.

2. I _____ a server.

3. They _____ chefs.

4. You _____ from London.

5. He _____ a writer.

6. We _____ artists.

2 Make the sentences negative.

1. He's from Seoul.

   _He isn't from Seoul._____

2. I'm an artist.

   _____

3. His name is Hiroshi.

   _____

4. You're in my class.

   _____

5. Beth and I are singers.

   _____

6. Mara and Charlie are from the US.

   _____

3 Write questions and answers about the people in the photos.
Use the words in parentheses.

1. (server?)

   _Is he a server_____?

   _No, he isn't._____. _He's a chef._____.

2. (teacher?)

   _____?

   _____. _____.

3. (web designers?)

   _____?

   _____. _____.

4. (businesswoman?)

   _____?

   _____. _____.

4 Correct the sentences.

1. I̶ a businessman. ✗

   I'm a businessman.

2. Bill a̶m̶ from the US. ✗

   _____

3. She'̶s̶ ̶w̶e̶b̶ ̶d̶e̶s̶i̶g̶n̶e̶r̶. ✗

   _____

4. I n̶o̶ ̶a̶m̶ from London. ✗

   _____

5. A̶r̶e̶ he a singer? ✗

   _____

6. Y̶o̶u̶ from Toronto? ✗

   _____

5 Choose the sentences from the box to complete the conversation.

> Are you from San Francisco
> I'm a teacher
> I'm from Chicago
> I'm Sue
> M̶y̶ ̶n̶a̶m̶e̶'̶s̶ ̶M̶a̶r̶k̶

Mark   Hi. ¹ My name's Mark _____.

Sue   Hello, Mark. Nice to meet you.

        ² _____.

Mark   ³ _____, Sue?

Sue   Yes, I am. How about you?

Mark   ⁴ _____. Are you a student here?

Sue   No, ⁵ _____.

6 Read the conversation in Activity 5 again. Write a similar conversation. Use the information on the list.

> # Guests
>
> | Name | Job | From |
> |------|-----|------|
> | Tom Anderson | writer | US |
> | Sally Atkins | actor | Canada |

Tom   Hi. ¹ My name's _____ Tom.

Sally   Hello, Tom. ² I'm Sally _____.

Tom   ³ _____ Canada?

Sally   ⁴ _____. How about you?

Tom   ⁵ _____. ⁶ _____ a writer?

Sally   No, ⁷ _____.

LISTENING

GO ONLINE Go to www.smartchoicepractice.com. Download the audio for Unit 1.

🔊**1** Listen. Match the conversations (1–2) and the pictures (A–B).

1. ——

2. ——

A.

B.

🔊**2** Listen again. Choose (✓) *True* or *False*.

	True	False
1. Bill isn't a chef.	☐	✓
2. Sara is a server.	☐	☐
3. Sara isn't from New York.	☐	☐
4. Bill is from Miami.	☐	☐
5. Katie and Jonah are from Los Angeles.	☐	☐
6. Katie is an actor.	☐	☐
7. Jonah isn't a model.	☐	☐

PRONUNCIATION

🔊**1** Listen. Choose (✓) *a* or *an*.

	a	an
1.	✓	☐
2.	☐	☐
3.	☐	☐
4.	☐	☐
5.	☐	☐
6.	☐	☐

READING

1 Match the photos (1–4) and texts (A–D).

Photo 1 – Text _B_   Photo 2 – Text ____   Photo 3 – Text ____   Photo 4 – Text ____

A
> Young-hee Kim is from Seoul in South Korea. She's a teacher in a large school.

B
> This is Atasuke Nakamura. He's from Nagasaki in Japan. Atasuke is a chef in a sushi restaurant.

C
> Fred Bevan is a businessman. He's from Toronto, Canada.

D
> This is Fernanda Leal. She's a tour guide from Brazil.

2 Read the texts again. Correct the sentences below.

1. Young-hee is from Taiwan. ✗

   Young-hee isn't from Taiwan . _She's from South Korea_ .

2. Fernanda is a businesswoman. ✗

   _____ . _____ .

3. Fred is from Montreal. ✗

   _____ . _____ .

4. Atasuke is an engineer. ✗

   _____ . _____ .

5. Fernanda is from Mexico. ✗

   _____ . _____ .

6. Young-hee is a programmer. ✗

   _____ . _____ .

VOCABULARY

1 Complete the sentences. Use the words in the box.

address	birthday	email address	major	favorite food
hometown	~~name~~	phone number	hobby	favorite singer

1. My _____name_____ is Sandy.

2. My _____ is 105 Main Street.

3. My _____ is 583-8710.

4. My _____ is sandy12@yoohoo.com.

5. My _____ is Mexico City.

6. My _____ is May 27th.

7. My _____ is pizza.

8. My _____ is chemistry.

9. My _____ is Taylor Swift.

10. My _____ is running.

2 Read the sentences in Activity **1** again. Write similar sentences about you.

1. HELLO! Me   My name is _____

2. _____

3. _____

4. _____

LANGUAGE PRACTICE

1 Complete the chart. Use the words in the box.

her	his	its	~~my~~	our	their	your	your

I	you	he	she	it	we	you	they
my							

2 Look at the pictures and business cards. Complete the sentences.

Peter Clark
14 Sandford Square
Boston, MA
Tel: 525-8714
artist

Mary Gordon
Writer
36 Oak Street
Sydney 2010
Tel: 792-1474

1. _His name is_ Peter Clark.

2. _____ Mary Gordon.

3. _____ 792-1474.

4. _____ 14 Sandford Square.

5. _____ 525-8714.

6. _____ 36 Oak Street.

3 Write questions and answers about Jennifer Lawrence. Use the information in the profile and the words in parentheses.

1. (nickname) _What's her nickname?_ ?

    Her nickname is Jen.

2. (birthday) _____ ?

    _____

3. (hobby) _____ ?

    _____

4. (from) _____ ?

    _____

5. (favorite food) _____ ?

    _____

Star profile

Name: Jennifer Shrader Lawrence

Nickname: Jen

Birthday: August 15th

Hobby: playing guitar

From: Louisville, Kentucky, US

Favorite food: French fries

4 Correct the sentences.

1. ~~What~~ your telephone number? ✗

   _What's your telephone number?_____

2. ~~What's~~ your birthday? ✗

   _____

3. Who ~~are~~ your favorite actor? ✗

   _____

4. What's ~~you're~~ major? ✗

   _____

5 Complete the conversation. Use the questions in the box.

How about you	How about you
~~when's your birthday~~	What's your hobby
Who's your favorite singer	where are you from

Dave   Happy birthday, Rita!

Rita   Thank you!

        So, [1] _when's your birthday_____, Dave?

Dave   It's June 21st.

Rita   And [2] _____?

Dave   I'm from California. [3] _____?

Rita   I'm from Brazil. [4] _____?

Dave   Listening to music.

Rita   Really? My hobby is listening to music, too!

Dave   Wow! [5] _____?

Rita   Beyoncé. [6] _____?

Dave   My favorite singer is Adam Levine.

6 Complete the questions. Use *what, when, where,* or *who.* Then answer the questions with information about you.

1. _What____'s your nickname?   _My nickname is_____

2. _____'s your favorite singer?   _____

3. _____ are you from?   _____

4. _____'s your birthday?   _____

LISTENING

GO

ONLINE Go to www.smartchoicepractice.com. Download the audio for Unit 2.

1 Listen to the conversations. Number the pictures.

A.

B.

C.

2 Listen again. Choose the best anwer to complete each sentence.

1. The information in the tennis club directory is ___.
   a. phone number and birthday
   b. phone number and email address
   c. email address and hometown

2. Senji's email address is ___.
   a. senji.tanaka@go.net
   b. senji_tanaka@go.net
   c. senji-tanaka@go.net

3. Senji's phone number is ___.
   a. 535-555-7274
   b. 535-555-7247
   c. 535-555-9727

4. Violeta's email address is ___.
   a. v_on@yoohoo.com
   b. v_ahn@yoohoo.com
   c. v.ahn@yoohoo.com

5. Ana's email address is ___.
   a. anadotmorales@go.net
   b. ana-morales@go.net
   c. ana.morales@go.net

PRONUNCIATION

1 Listen to the phone numbers. Mark (-) the pauses between the numbers.

1. 5 3 5 - 5 5 5 - 7 2 7 4
2. 5 3 5 5 5 5 7 2 4 7
3. 3 7 1 5 5 5 0 2 3 1
4. 2 4 4 3 5 5 0 6 2 9
5. 2 4 4 3 5 0 6 2 9

2 Listen again. Practice reading the phone numbers. Pause between the groups of numbers.

READING

1 **Read the text quickly. Choose the correct answers.**

1. Rosana is a (teacher / student).

2. George is (Rosana's teacher / a student).

To: Rosana Gomes <rgomes378@ucla.edu>

From: George Jones <g.jones@martinsweb.net>

Subject: I'm here!

Hi, George!

How are you? How are your classes? Hey, I'm in Los Angeles! I'm an English major at UCLA now. The university is very interesting, and my teachers are great. One of my teachers is a famous writer! Also, I'm in the university's photography club and tennis club. They are so fun!

What's your address? Is it 314 Jackson Avenue, Los Angeles? By the way, my phone number is 559-7825 and my email address is rgomes378@ucla.edu.

Let's meet up!

Rosana

---

2 **Read the text again. Answer the questions.**

1. Where is Rosana?

   She's in Los Angeles.

2. Is George in Los Angeles?

   _____

3. What's Rosana's major?

   _____

4. Are Rosana's hobbies swimming and biking?

   _____

5. What's George's email address?

   _____

6. What's Rosana's phone number?

   _____

3 | That's my wallet!

VOCABULARY

1 Write the missing letters.

1. t _e_ x t _b_ o o _k_ s
2. d __ iv __ r's li __ __ n __ e
3. __ ell __ hon __
4. m __ n __ y
5. __ e a __ __ h __ n __ s
6. w __ l __ et
7. __ T M __ a r __
8. g __ a __ __ e s
9. __ e __ s

2 Label the photos. Use the words in Activity 1.

1. wallet

2. _____

3. _____

4. _____

5. _____

6. _____

7. _____

8. _____

9. _____

LANGUAGE PRACTICE

1 Complete the sentences. Use *this*, *that*, *these*, or *those*, and *is* or *are*.

1. _This is_____ my camera.

2. _____ my sisters.

3. _____ my keys.

4. _____ my son.

2 Put the words in the correct order to make questions. Then complete the answers.

1. this / is / cell phone / your

   A _Is this your cell phone?_____ ?

   B Yes, _it is_____ .

2. your / are / these / photos

   A _____ ?

   B No, _____. Those _____ my sister's photos.

3. that / dog / is / your

   A _____ ?

   B Yes, _____. This _____ Toby.

4. are / those / who / people

   A _____ ?

   B _____ my friends Beth and Larry.

3 Correct the sentences.

1. ~~Are~~ this your camera? ✗

   <u>Is this your camera?</u>

2. Is ~~those~~ your car? ✗

   _____

3. ~~This~~ your wallet? ✗

   _____

4. A Are these her parents?

   B Yes, ~~these~~ are. ✗

   _____

4 Complete the conversation. Use the words in the box.

They're	~~Who are~~	is this	it isn't	is that

Carl   Is this your photo, Maria?

Maria   Yes, it is.

Carl   ¹ <u>Who are</u> these boys?

Maria   ² _____ my brothers, Pete and Kevin.

Carl   And ³ _____ your sister?

Maria   No, ⁴ _____. That's my mother! Her name's Laura.

Carl   And ⁵ _____ your mother's new computer?

Maria   Yes, it is.

5 Look at Henry's photo. Read the conversation in Activity 4 again. Write a similar conversation.

Henry   Is this your photo, Sharon?

Sharon   Yes, ¹ <u>it is</u>.

Henry   ² _____ girls?

Sharon   ³ _____, Jessica and Molly.

Henry   And ⁴ _____ brother?

Sharon   No, ⁵ _____.

   ⁶ _____ father!

   His name's Jeremy.

Henry   And ⁷ _____ car?

Sharon   Yes, ⁸ _____.

LISTENING

GO ONLINE
Go to www.smartchoicepractice.com. Download the audio for Unit 3.

◀)) **1** Listen to the conversations. Number the pictures.

A. ☐

B. 1

C. ☐

D. ☐

◀)) **2** Listen again. Choose the correct answer.

1. Skippy is the name of (the dog / Pete's brother).
2. Sam's phone number is (209-7312 / 209-3712).
3. It's a photo of Linda's (parents / grandparents).
4. Kim and Tara are in a (blue / red) car.

PRONUNCIATION

◀)) **1** Listen to parts of the conversation again. Write the missing numbers.

1. **B** He's __13__ years old.

   A Wow! That's old!

2. **A** And what's your address?

   B My address is _____ Oak Street.

3. **A** What's your email address?

   B It's Sam_____@yoohoo.com.

4. **A** How old are they?

   B Let's see… my grandmother is _____ and my grandfather is 82.

5. **A** How old are they?

   B Kim is _____ and Tara is _____.

14

READING

1 Read the text quickly. What does everybody have in their bag? Select (✓) the boxes.

☐ a wallet   ☐ textbooks   ☐ headphones   ☐ money

☐ a cell phone   ☐ keys   ☐ a school ID card   ☐ a driver's license

Take a Look
What's in your bag?

This is our school. And these are the students from our school. Today's question is… What's in *your* bag?

Interviewer: Excuse me, James!

James: Yes?

Interviewer: What's in your bag?

James: Well, this is my cell phone, and this is my wallet.

Interviewer: What's in your wallet?

James: My driver's license and some money.

Interviewer: Thank you… And Kate! Is this your blue bag?

Kate: Yes, it is.

Interviewer: What's in it?

Kate: Well, these are my textbooks. And this is my cell phone, and this is my school ID card.

Interviewer: Thanks, Kate. Excuse me, Brendan!

Brendan: Yes?

Interviewer: What's in your bag?

Brendan: Well, these are my glasses, and this is my cell phone. Oh, and this is my wallet.

Interviewer: What's in your wallet?

Brendan: My school ID card.

Interviewer: Thank you! And how about you, Sophie? What's in your bag?

Sophie: These are my keys, and these are my headphones. And this is my cell phone.

Interviewer: Thank you!

2 Read the text again. Select (✓) the other things that each person has in his/her bag.

	1. James	2. Kate	3. Brendan	4. Sophie
a wallet	✓			
keys				
headphones				
money				
textbooks				
glasses				
a driver's license				
a school ID card				

VOCABULARY

1 Choose the best answers to complete the text.

> My name's Roberto Diaz.
>
> I'm ¹___ at Yale University.
>
> I'm ²___ Houston, Texas.
>
> My ³___ singer is Ed Sheeran.
>
> My ⁴___ is May 24th.
>
> My ⁵___ is 345-2957.

1. a. a student
   b. student
   c. chef
   d. an actor

2. a. about
   b. of
   c. from
   d. hometown

3. a. name
   b. favorite
   c. nickname
   d. major

4. a. birthday
   b. hobby
   c. address
   d. phone number

5. a. email address
   b. address
   c. type
   d. phone number

2 Choose the best answer to complete each sentence.

1. Bill Gates is ___.
   a. an actor
   b. a businessman
   c. a student
   d. an engineer

2. Brad Pitt is ___.
   a. a singer
   b. a chef
   c. a web designer
   d. an actor

3. J.K. Rowling is a ___.
   a. server
   b. writer
   c. teacher
   d. tour guide

4. A What's your ___?
   B 24 East Street.
   a. email address
   b. birthday
   c. address
   d. hobby

5. My ___ is chemistry.
   a. keys
   b. favorite color
   c. major
   d. glasses

6. A What's in your wallet?
   B ___.
   a. My glasses
   b. My cell phone
   c. Money
   d. Headphones

LANGUAGE

1 Choose the best answers to complete the text.

To: Ted
From: Alex
Subject: Hi!

Hi, Ted!

I'm in England! ¹____ at the Thames Language School. It's a great school. My teacher's name is Thomas, and ²____ really nice. ³____ is a photo of me and my friend Julia. She's from Taiwan, too. ⁴____ favorite singer is Taylor Swift. ⁵____ in London? ⁶____ your phone number?

Let's meet up!

Alex

1. a. I
   b. I'm
   c. Am
   d. My

2. a. her
   b. he
   c. he's
   d. his

3. a. It
   b. This
   c. Those
   d. These

4. a. His
   b. He's
   c. Her
   d. She's

5. a. You are
   b. You
   c. Is you
   d. Are you

6. a. What
   b. What's
   c. Where's
   d. Who's

2 Choose the best answer to complete each sentence.

1. Are ____ your parents?
   a. those
   b. this
   c. that
   d. it

2. A Are these your photos?
   B No, ____.
   a. they are
   b. they aren't
   c. it is
   d. it isn't

3. ____ Richard Fowler.
   a. Name is
   b. I'm name is
   c. My name is
   d. My name

4. ____ my cell phone.
   a. These are
   b. That
   c. This
   d. That's

5. ____ Matthew?
   a. Your name
   b. You name
   c. Name is
   d. Is your name

6. A ____
   B Yes, she is.
   a. Is she a teacher?
   b. Is she teacher?
   c. She teacher?
   d. Is her a teacher?

7. A Are you from Mexico?
   B ____
   a. Yes, I'm.
   b. Yes, I am.
   c. No, I not.
   d. No, I'm.

17

CONVERSATION

1 Choose the best sentence to complete each conversation.

1. A Nice to meet you.
   B _____
   a. No, it isn't.
   b. Nice to meet you, too.
   c. Great, thanks.
   d. How about you?

2. A _____
   B I'm from Miami.
   a. Where are you from?
   b. How are you?
   c. Nice to meet you.
   d. Where are you?

3. A How are you?
   B _____
   a. No, I'm not.
   b. Great, thanks.
   c. How are you?
   d. I'm Tom.

4. A _____
   B Yes, I am.
   a. Are you a student here?
   b. Is this your camera?
   c. How are you?
   d. What's your name?

5. A Is your name Steve?
   B _____
   a. No, it's not. It's Dave.
   b. No, it's not. It's Steve.
   c. Yes, it's steve@me.com.
   d. No, my hobby is swimming.

6. A _____
   B It's Martha Black.
   a. What's your address?
   b. What's your name?
   c. Where are you from?
   d. Are you Martha Black?

7. A _____
   B No, it's 589-4344.
   a. What's your phone number?
   b. My phone number is 589-4344.
   c. Is your email address pete@ ny.com?
   d. Is your phone number 589-4345?

8. A _____
   B They're my friends.
   a. Who is that girl?
   b. Are those your friends?
   c. Who are those people?
   d. Is she your mother?

9. A _____
   B Yes, it is.
   a. Is that your cell phone?
   b. Are these your keys?
   c. Are those your glasses?
   d. Are these your photos?

10. A _____
    B Blue.
    a. What's your name?
    b. What's your nickname?
    c. What's your major?
    d. What's your favorite color?

11. A When's your birthday?
    B _____
    a. Los Angeles.
    b. July 24th.
    c. It's really great.
    d. Yellow.

12. A How are you?
    B _____
    A Good, thanks.
    a. Great, thanks. Nice to meet you, too.
    b. Great, thanks. Me, too!
    c. Great, thanks. Is this your family?
    d. Great, thanks. How about you?

READING

1 Read the article. Choose the best answers.

This is a photo of Margaret Flynn. Margaret's nickname is Meg. She's an actor. She's from the town of Trenton, New Jersey. This photo is by Meg's favorite photographer Henri Arnaud. Arnaud is from Paris. Meg's father, Martin, is an actor, too, and her brother Glenn is a singer. Glenn is on tour now in New Orleans. His tour is from July 24th to August 5th.

Meg's in New York now. Her new movie *The Chef* opens there on August 4th. That's the actor's birthday.

1. Where's Meg from?
   a. New Orleans.
   b. Paris.
   c. New York.
   d. New Jersey.

2. Who's a photographer?
   a. Meg.
   b. Martin.
   c. Henri.
   d. Glenn.

3. Who's a singer?
   a. Glenn.
   b. Henri.
   c. Margaret.
   d. Martin.

4. Where's Glenn?
   a. In New Orleans.
   b. In New York.
   c. In New Jersey.
   d. In Paris.

5. Who's from Paris?
   a. Glenn.
   b. Henri.
   c. Margaret.
   d. Martin.

6. When is Meg's birthday?
   a. In May.
   b. In June.
   c. In July.
   d. In August.

VOCABULARY

1 What kind of music is it? Complete the label under each picture.

1. j a z z

2. __ __ __ – h __ __ __

3. __ l __ __ __ __ __ __ __ __ __ a

4. __ __ __ k __ __ __ __ __ c

5. d __ __ __ __
   __ __ __ __ c

6. __ __ __ s __ __ __ __ __
   m __ __ __ __

2 What's your favorite kind of music? What about your family? Complete the sentences. Use the words in Activity 1 or your own ideas.

1. My favorite kind of music is _____.

2. My _____'s favorite kind of music is _____.

3. My _____'s favorite kind of music is _____.

LANGUAGE PRACTICE

1 Complete Don's sentences. Use *is*, the words in the box, and the information in parentheses.

amazing	not bad	~~OK~~	OK	good	terrible

1. Classical music _is OK_____. (★☆☆☆)

2. Rock music _____. (★★★☆)

3. Electronica _____. (☆☆☆☆)

4. Latin music _____. (★★★★)

5. Dance music _____. (★★☆☆)

6. Pop music _____. (★☆☆☆)

2 Complete the sentences. Use negative (–) or affirmative (+) forms of *like*.

1. Helen and Simon _don't like_ (–) pop music. They _like___ (+) rock.

2. My brother _____ (–) electronica. He _____ (+) Latin music.

3. Paula and I _____ (–) hip-hop. We _____ (+) electronica.

4. I _____ (+) rock music. I _____ (–) jazz.

5. You _____ (+) classical music. You _____ (–) Latin music.

6. Susanna _____ (–) dance music. She _____ (+) jazz.

3 Write questions. Use *like* and the words in parentheses. Then answer the questions. Use the information in parentheses.

1. (Steve / Latin music) _Does Steve like Latin music_____?

   (☺) _Yes, he does_____.

2. (Carla / dance music) _____?

   (☺) _____.

3. (Steve and Carla / electronica) _____?

   (☹) _____.

4. (Steve / the piano) _____?

   (☹) _____.

4 Write questions about the people in parentheses. Use *What kind of ... ?* Answer with the information in the chart.

	Josh	Lisa
jazz	✓	
Latin music		✓
pop music		✓
dance music	✓	✓
hip-hop	✓	

1. (Josh) <u>What kind of music does Josh like</u> ?

   <u>He</u>

2. (Lisa) _____?

   _____

3. (Josh and Lisa) _____?

   _____

5 Correct the sentences.

1. I ~~not~~ like jazz. ✗

   <u>I don't like jazz.</u>

2. ~~Like you~~ pop music? ✗

   _____

3. What kind of music ~~you~~ like? ✗

   _____

4. A Do you like the guitar?

   B Yes, I ~~like~~. ✗

   _____

6 Complete the conversation. Use the words in the box.

~~Do you like~~	don't like	I don't	Me, too	What about	What kind of

Matt   Let's listen to some music.

        ¹ <u>Do you like</u> hip-hop?

Jackie No, ² _____.

Matt   What about rock music?

Jackie No, I ³ _____ rock music.

        ⁴ _____ dance music?

Matt   No, I don't like dance music.

        ⁵ _____ music do you like?

Jackie I like jazz and Latin music.

Matt   ⁶ _____. Let's listen

        to Enrique Iglesias.

LISTENING

GO ONLINE Go to www.smartchoicepractice.com. Download the audio for Unit 4.

🔊**1** Listen to the conversation. Where are they? Choose (✓) the correct picture.

A. ☐

B. ☐

🔊**2** Listen again. Choose (✓) *True* or *False.*

	True	False
1. It is Tom's music.	☐	☐
2. Tom's brother doesn't like hip-hop.	☐	☐
3. Alice likes hip-hop.	☐	☐
4. Tom thinks rock music is annoying.	☐	☐
5. Tom loves the trumpet.	☐	☐
6. Alice and Tom like jazz.	☐	☐

PRONUNCIATION

🔊**1** Listen to the questions. Mark the intonation above the questions.

1. Is this your music?

2. Does your brother like hip-hop?

3. Is this the new Jay-Z song?

4. Do you like hip-hop?

5. Do you like rock music?

6. Does your brother like jazz?

READING

1 Read the text quickly. Match the two parts of the sentences.

1. Akiko is from ___
2. Cathy is from ___
3. Ben is from ___

a. England.
b. Japan.
c. the US.

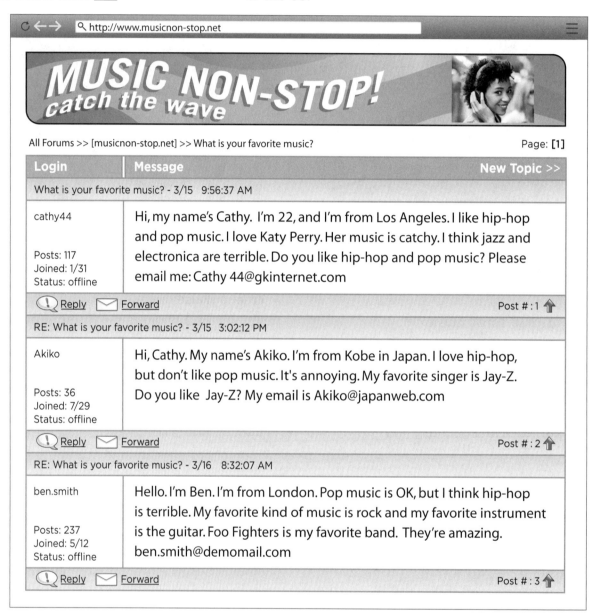

2 Read the text again. Complete the chart.

	Cathy	Akiko	Ben
Favorite kind of music	1 hip-hop pop music	4	7
Favorite band/ singer	2	5	8
Doesn't like	3	6	9

5 / What do you do for fun?

VOCABULARY

1 Complete the activities with the verbs in the box.

do	go	have	listen	~~play~~	watch

1. __play__ video games
2. _____ TV
3. _____ to music
4. _____ shopping
5. _____ coffee with friends
6. _____ yoga

2 Label the pictures. Use the phrases in Activity 1.

1. _____ _do yoga_ _____   2. _____   3. _____

4. _____   5. _____   6. _____

LANGUAGE PRACTICE

1 **Complete the sentences. Use the simple present affirmative of the verbs in the box.**

| do | go | have | listen | play | watch |

1. Phil _does_ yoga.

2. I _____ to music on Saturdays.

3. We _____ soccer on Tuesday night.

4. Eva _____ TV with her friends.

5. You _____ shopping on Mondays.

6. They _____ coffee with their friends every Sunday.

2 **Make the sentences from Activity 1 negative.**

1. _Phil doesn't do yoga._

2. _____

3. _____

4. _____

5. _____

6. _____

3 **Read the survey forms. Write questions and answers.**

Name: Amanda Lewis		
Free-time activities:	Yes	No
have coffee with friends	●	○
go shopping	●	○
listen to music	○	●
watch movies	●	○
watch TV	○	●
play video games	●	○
play tennis	●	○
do yoga	●	○

Name: Diego Villa		
Free-time activities:	Yes	No
have coffee with friends	●	○
go shopping	○	●
listen to music	○	●
watch movies	●	○
watch TV	●	○
play video games	○	●
play soccer	●	○
do yoga	○	●

1. (Amanda / do yoga?)   _Does Amanda do yoga_ ?

   Yes, she does .

2. (Diego / go shopping?)   _____ ?

   _____ .

3. (Amanda and Diego / watch movies?)   _____ ?

   _____ .

4. (Diego / have coffee with friends?)   _____ ?

   _____ .

5. (Amanda / play video games?)   _____ ?

   _____ .

4 Put the words in order to make questions. Then match the questions and answers.

1. When / Diego / does / watch TV / ?

   <u>When does Diego watch TV?</u>   <u>b</u>   **a.** At the mall.

2. Diego / Where / play soccer / does / ?

   _____ ___   **b.** At night.

3. does / Amanda / play / What / ?

   _____ ___   **c.** Tennis.

4. go shopping / does / Amanda / Where / ?

   _____ ___   **d.** At school.

5 Complete the conversation. Use the words in the box.

| ~~Do you play~~ | I do | like | I play | you play |

Chris   ¹ <u>Do you play</u> soccer?

Anita   Yes, ² _____. How about you?

        Do ³ _____ soccer?

Chris   No, but I play tennis. And I ⁴ _____ video games.

Anita   Really?

Chris   Yeah, ⁵ _____ video games every night.

Anita   Wow! You really like video games!

6 Write true sentences about you and your best friend. Use the affirmative or negative of the simple present and the words in parentheses.

1. (do yoga)

   <u>I do yoga. / I don't do yoga.</u>

   <u>My best friend does yoga. / My best friend doesn't do yoga.</u>

2. (play soccer)

   _____

   _____

3. (watch movies)

   _____

   _____

LISTENING

GO ONLINE Go to www.smartchoicepractice.com. Download the audio for Unit 5.

1 Listen to the conversation. Select (✓) the activities you hear.

1. ☐ play soccer
2. ☐ do yoga
3. ☐ shop online
4. ☐ watch TV
5. ☐ play video games
6. ☐ download an app

2 Listen again. Choose (✓) *True* or *False*.

	True	False
1. Mike doesn't do yoga.	✓	☐
2. Tara does yoga.	☐	☐
3. Tara does yoga at home.	☐	☐
4. Mike doesn't play video games.	☐	☐
5. Tara's favorite video game is Fire Ring.	☐	☐
6. Mike doesn't like Fire Ring.	☐	☐
7. Mike and Tara are free on Thursday.	☐	☐
8. Mike is free on Friday.	☐	☐

PRONUNCIATION

1 Listen to the questions. Choose (✓) *rising intonation* (_____) or *falling intonation* (_____).

	rising	falling
1.	✓	☐
2.	☐	☐
3.	☐	☐
4.	☐	☐
5.	☐	☐
6.	☐	☐
7.	☐	☐
8.	☐	☐

READING

1 Read the text quickly. Select (✓) the activities mentioned.

1. ✓ read books
2. ☐ have coffee
3. ☐ play soccer
4. ☐ play tennis
5. ☐ upload videos
6. ☐ send text messages
7. ☐ go shopping
8. ☐ shop online
9. ☐ go to the movies

Dear Melissa,

How are you?

Monica and I are in Chicago. We're at a language school. The school is OK, and our teacher is really great. His name's Andy, and he's from Miami. He's amazing. He likes all kinds of music and knows a lot about them.

We don't have classes on Saturdays and Sundays, so we have some free time. On Saturdays, we go shopping and have coffee with some classmates. On Sundays, I play tennis with a friend from school. Monica doesn't like tennis, so she stays home and reads books or shops online. Sometimes we go dancing or go to the movies.

See you soon.

Love,

Antonella

2 Read the text again. Complete the sentences with the correct names.

1. _Monica and Antonella_ are in Chicago.
2. _____ is from Miami.
3. _____ likes all kinds of music.
4. _____ have coffee with classmates.
5. _____ plays tennis on Sundays.
6. _____ shops online on Sundays.

6 / Can you play the guitar?

VOCABULARY

1 Look at the pictures. Complete the crossword with the correct activities.

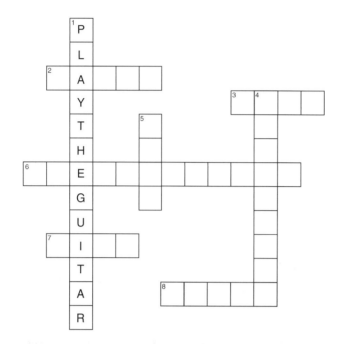
1.

2.

3.

4.

5.

6.

7.

8.

2 Answer the questions with information about you.

1. Do you cook dinner?

   Yes, I do. / No, I don't.

2. Do you drive to school?

3. Do you ride a bike to school?

4. Do you play the guitar?

30

LANGUAGE PRACTICE

1 **Complete the sentences. Use *can* or *can't* and the words in parentheses.**

1. Raul and Dora _can dance_____ well. (dance / ☺)

2. Donna _____ very well. (play soccer / ☺)

3. Toby _____. (ride a bike / ☹)

4. They _____ very well. (draw / ☺)

5. Lisa _____ at all. (sing / ☹)

6. Jodie _____ very well. (cook / ☹)

2 **Look at the chart. Write questions and answers about Stan and Laura.**

Stan		Laura
✓	cook?	✓
✗	sing?	✓
✗	play the guitar?	✗
✓	ride a bike?	✓
✓	drive?	✓

1. (Stan and Laura / cook)   _Can Stan and Laura cook_____ ?

                                 _Yes, they can._____ .

2. (Stan / sing)   _____ ?

                                 _____ .

3. (Stan and Laura / play the guitar)   _____ ?

                                 _____ .

4. (Stan / ride a bike)   _____ ?

                                 _____ .

5. (Laura / drive)   _____ ?

                                 _____ .

3 **Correct the sentences.**

1. I can ~~to draw~~. ✗

   I can draw.

2. He can't ~~dances~~. ✗

   _____

3. She can ~~very well drive~~. ✗

   _____

4. They ~~don't can~~ ride a bike. ✗

   _____

5. What ~~you can~~ do? ✗

   _____

6. **A** Can he sing?

   B Yes, he ~~do~~. ✗

   _____

4 **Complete the conversation. Use the sentences in the box.**

> Can you play soccer?
> Can you ride a bike?
> Yes, I can.
> ~~What can you do, Kylie?~~

Eric ¹ _What can you do, Kylie?_

Kylie I can draw.

Eric Really? ² _____

Kylie No, I can't.

Eric ³ _____

Kylie ⁴ _____

Let's play a game!

Eric Uh, sorry. I can't play soccer at all.

5 **Complete the questions. Then answer with information about you.**

1. _Can_ you drive?

   _____.

2. Can you _____ the guitar?

   _____.

3. Can you _____ a bike?

   _____.

4. _____ you play tennis?

   _____.

5. What can you _____?

   _____.

LISTENING

GO
ONLINE Go to www.smartchoicepractice.com. Download the audio for Unit 6.

1 Listen. Where are they? Choose (✓) the correct picture.

A.

B.

C.

D.

2 Listen again. What can they do? Select (✓) the boxes.

Brett	Activity	Terry
	play the guitar	
	play the piano	
	sing	
	dance	

PRONUNCIATION

1 Listen to the questions and answers. Choose (✓) *can* or *can't*.

	can	can't
1.	✓	
2.		
3.		
4.		
5.		
6.		
7.		
8.		

READING

1 Read the text quickly. Answer the questions.

1. Does Marina go to school in Boston? _____

2. Does she like Carlos Santana? _____

3. Does she like cars? _____

4. Does she play tennis at a club? _____

AND SHE CAN PLAY THE GUITAR, TOO!

Marina Sanchez is a student at the Juilliard School, the famous music school in New York. Marina can play the guitar very well. She can sing very well, too. "But I can't dance," she says, "so I don't think I can be a pop singer, right? Well, I don't like pop music very much, anyway. But I like Latin music. Carlos Santana is one of my favorite musicians."

Marina has classes from Monday to Friday. She can't drive, so she rides a bike to school. "I can't drive, but I like cars. My favorite cars are Porsches and Ferraris." On Saturdays and Sundays, she plays tennis in the neighborhood. "I can't play tennis very well," she says, "so I need to practice."

2 Read the text again. Complete the sentences about Marina. Use *can* or *can't*.

1. She _can_ play the guitar.

2. She _____ sing.

3. She _____ dance.

4. She _____ drive.

5. She _____ ride a bike.

6. She _____ play tennis very well.

VOCABULARY

1 Choose the best answers to complete the text.

Come to the East Village Activity Center!

On Mondays, we play ¹___.
On Tuesdays, we ²___ yoga.
On Wednesdays, we ³___ bikes.
On Thursdays, we play ⁴___.
On Fridays, we dance and sing.
Can you play ⁵___?

1. a. shopping
   b. videos
   c. tennis
   d. yoga

2. a. do
   b. go
   c. can
   d. are

3. a. drive
   b. play
   c. do
   d. ride

4. a. dance
   b. soccer
   c. yoga
   d. bikes

5. a. the bike
   b. the movies
   c. the computer
   d. the piano

2 Choose the best answer to complete each sentence.

1. I don't like electronica. It's ___!
   a. terrible
   b. catchy
   c. not bad
   d. amazing

2. I like jazz. It's ___!
   a. terrible
   b. boring
   c. annoying
   d. pleasant

3. Can you ___ videos?
   a. ride
   b. drive
   c. upload
   d. do

4. Let's ___ shopping.
   a. have
   b. read
   c. go
   d. play

5. I don't watch ___.
   a. TV
   b. video games
   c. music
   d. books

6. Can you ___?
   a. go French
   b. play French
   c. speak French
   d. dance French

7. I can sing ___.
   a. amazing
   b. terrible
   c. at all
   d. very well

LANGUAGE

1 **Choose the best answers to complete the text.**

For fun, Judy Williams [1]___ soccer in the neighborhood on Fridays and tennis at a club on Sundays. Her sisters, Pam and Lara, [2]___ sports. Pam [3]___ music. She can [4]___ the guitar very well. And Lara [5]___ computers. She [6]___ every day. But they all love shopping. They go shopping together every Saturday.

1. a. play
   b. plays
   c. is
   d. can

2. a. does
   b. do
   c. doesn't like
   d. don't like

3. a. like
   b. do
   c. likes
   d. doesn't

4. a. play
   b. plays
   c. does
   d. do

5. a. like
   b. do
   c. likes
   d. does

6. a. do
   b. does
   c. send emails
   d. sends emails

2 **Choose the best answer to complete each sentence.**

1. She ___ soccer on Saturdays.
   a. not play
   b. doesn't plays
   c. doesn't play
   d. don't play

2. I ___ like pop music.
   a. no
   b. am not
   c. doesn't
   d. don't

3. What ___ do on Sundays?
   a. do you
   b. you
   c. do
   d. are you

4. A Do you shop online?
   B ___
   a. Yes, I shops.
   b. Yes, I do.
   c. Yes, I does.
   d. Yes, I am.

5. ___ use a computer?
   a. Can you to
   b. Are you can
   c. Do you can
   d. Can you

6. What ___?
   a. can do
   b. can she do
   c. can she to do
   d. can she does

CONVERSATION

1 Choose the best sentence to complete each conversation.

1. **A** I don't like jazz.
   B _____
   a. Me, too. I like jazz.
   b. Really? I like jazz.
   c. Well, let's go to a concert.
   d. No, not really.

2. **A** Latin music is catchy.
   B _____
   a. Yeah, it's great.
   b. Yeah, it's terrible.
   c. Great. Thanks.
   d. Yes, she is.

3. **A** Let's go to a concert.
   B _____
   a. It's OK.
   b. Not bad, thanks.
   c. Great idea!
   d. Great, thanks.

4. **A** I like rock music.
   B _____
   a. No, I don't.
   b. Great idea!
   c. How about you?
   d. Me, too.

5. **A** _____
   B I play soccer.
   a. Do you like music?
   b. When do you play soccer?
   c. What do you do for fun?
   d. Do you play soccer on Fridays?

6. **A** When do you play video games?
   B _____
   a. Do you like video games?
   b. Yes, I do.
   c. In the neighborhood.
   d. On Saturdays.

7. **A** Can you drive?
   B _____
   a. No, I don't.
   b. Yes, you do.
   c. Yes, I can.
   d. No, you can't.

8. **A** _____
   B No, not really.
   a. What can you do?
   b. What's your favorite kind of music?
   c. Where do you go to relax with your friends?
   d. Can you dance?

9. **A** What can you do?
   B _____
   a. I can play the guitar.
   b. No, I can't.
   c. Yes, I do.
   d. I do yoga on Fridays.

10. **A** Can you sing?
    B _____
    a. Yes, you can.
    b. No, but I can sing.
    c. No, I can't sing at all.
    d. No, you can't sing.

11. **A** _____
    B I like pop.
    a. Can you dance?
    b. What kind of music do you like?
    c. Me, too.
    d. Really?

12. **A** Do you like classical music?
    B _____
    a. Let's go to a concert.
    b. No, not really.
    c. No, I not.
    d. Yes, I can.

READING

1 **Read the text. Choose the best answers.**

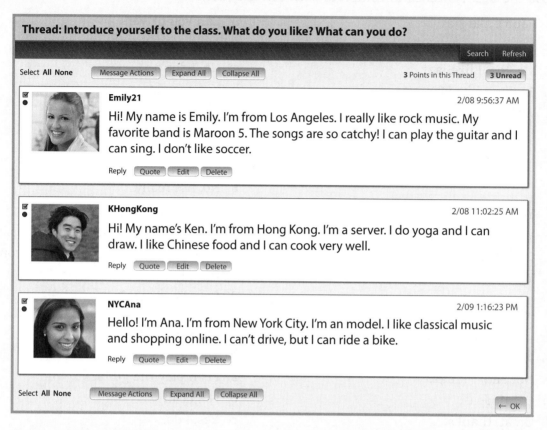

1. Where's Emily from?
   a. Los Angeles.
   b. Houston.
   c. Hong Kong.
   d. New York City.

2. What can Emily do?
   a. She can sing and dance.
   b. She can drive.
   c. She can sing and play the guitar.
   d. She can cook.

3. What is Ken's job?
   a. He's a programmer.
   b. He's a server.
   c. He's a chef.
   d. He's an artist.

4. What kind of food does Ken like?
   a. Chinese.
   b. Spanish.
   c. Italian.
   d. French.

5. Ana ____.
   a. is a tour guide
   b. likes shopping online
   c. doesn't like classical music
   d. can't ride a bike

6. Ana ____.
   a. can drive
   b. can't drive
   c. drives to work
   d. rides a bike every day

VOCABULARY

1 Find nine more clothing items in the word square.

K	D	S	H	O	R	T	S	E	F
T	D	W	G	U	I	L	A	D	V
S	N	E	A	K	E	R	S	Q	J
H	W	A	H	P	C	G	U	I	S
I	E	T	D	A	S	K	I	R	T
R	J	E	A	N	S	N	T	E	R
T	I	R	K	T	A	W	T	F	L
B	O	O	T	S	P	K	A	J	W
S	U	N	G	L	A	S	S	E	S

2 Write sentences about you. Use *wear* or *don't wear* and clothing items from Activity 1.

1. <u>I wear pants. / I don't wear pants.</u>

2. _____

3. _____

4. _____

LANGUAGE PRACTICE

1 Complete the sentences. Use the present continuous affirmative of the verbs in parentheses.

1. Jake _is playing_ the guitar. (play)

2. I _____. (dance)

3. You _____ to music. (listen)

4. Joel and Adam _____. (swim)

5. Patricia _____ a blue skirt. (wear)

6. Janet and I _____ pizza. (eat)

2 Make the sentences from Activity 1 negative.

1. _Jake isn't playing the guitar._   4. _____

2. _____   5. _____

3. _____   6. _____

3 Look at the picture. Write questions and answers. Use the present continuous.

1. (what / Teresa / do ?)

   What is Teresa doing?

   She's reading a magazine.

2. (Teresa / wear / jeans ?)

   _____

   _____

3. (Joe / eat / a hamburger ?)

   _____

   _____

4. (what / Joe / wear ?)

   _____

   _____

5. (Beth and Doug / dance ?)

   _____

   _____

6. (what / Beth and Doug / do ?)

   _____

   _____

4 Correct the sentences.

1. I ~~reading~~ ✗

   I'm reading.

2. ~~We's~~ watching TV. ✗

   _____

3. Alex ~~don't~~ using a computer. ✗

   _____

4. I ~~no am~~ playing soccer. ✗

   _____

5. Is she ~~wear~~ a purple sweater? ✗

   _____

6. What ~~do~~ you doing? ✗

   _____

5 Complete the conversation. Use the words and letters in the box.

am	~~having~~	's	's	's	's	's	's playing	's talking	's wearing	see

James   Hi, Erica. This is a great party!
        Are you ¹ _having_ fun?

Erica   Yes, I ² _____. Hey,
        where ³ _____ Harry?

James   He ⁴ _____ to Kate.

Erica   Oh, yes. I can ⁵ _____ him.

James   Who ⁶ _____ that girl
        over there?

Erica   Which girl?

James   That girl. She ⁷ _____ jeans and a red T-shirt.
        And she ⁸ _____ the guitar.

Erica   Oh, that ⁹ _____ Christina. She ¹⁰ _____ in
        my class.

James   She ¹¹ _____ really good at the guitar!

6 Put the words in order to make questions. Then answer the questions about you.

1. watching / your / is / teacher / TV / ?

   Is your teacher watching TV?

   Yes, she is. / No, she isn't.

2. wearing / what / you / are / ?

   _____

   _____

3. doing / what / your / are / friends / ?

   _____

   _____

LISTENING

GO
ONLINE Go to www.smartchoicepractice.com. Download the audio for Unit 7.

◀))**1** Listen. Where are they? Choose (✓) the correct place for each person.

	home	gym	school
1. Daria			✓
2. Maria			
3. Tony			
4. Andrew			

◀))**2** Listen again. Choose the best answer to complete each sentence.

1. Daria is ___.

    a. sending text messages

    b. talking on the phone and doing homework

    c. shopping online

2. Maria is ___.

    a. doing homework

    b. watching TV

    c. listening to music

3. Tony is ___.

    a. wearing athletic clothes

    b. buying business clothes

    c. talking on the phone

4. Andrew is ___.

    a. shopping online

    b. listening to music

    c. doing homework

5. Andrew is buying ___.

    a. athletic clothes

    b. business clothes

    c. trendy clothes

6. ___ is calling Andrew.

    a. Tony

    b. Maria

    c. Andrew's mom

PRONUNCIATION

◀))**1** Listen to the questions. Write the missing words.

1. _What are you_ doing?

2. What _____ is she listening to?

3. _____ doing?

4. _____ buying?

READING

1 Read the messages quickly. Choose the correct names.

1. *Vince / Wendy* is at home.
2. *Vince / Wendy* is at a coffee shop.

> Hi, Vince. Are you at home?

> Yes, I am.

> What are you doing?

> I'm uploading videos and sending text messages.

> Are Debbie and Ed there?

> Yes. Debbie is cooking tonight and Ed is helping her. Where are you? What are you doing?

> I'm at a coffee shop with Louis.

> Is he doing homework?

> No. He's reading books. They have some cool books here. And we're listening to this guy, David Guetta. He's a great singer. Do you know him?

> No, I don't. Is he from the US?

> No, he's from France. Check out his songs on his website.

> Ok. Thanks for the tip. Time to go. Talk to you later.

> OK. Bye.

2 Read the messages again. Answer the questions.

1. Is Vince writing messages?

   Yes, he is.

2. Is Debbie uploading videos?

   _____

3. What is Ed doing?

   _____

4. Is Wendy cooking?

   _____

5. What's Louis doing?

   _____

6. Who's Wendy listening to?

   _____

VOCABULARY

1 Look at the pictures. Complete the crossword.

Across

Down

2 Think about two rooms in your home. Which items from Activity 1 do you have?

In the _bedroom_ :

bed,

In the _____ :

_____

LANGUAGE PRACTICE

1 Look at the picture. Complete the sentences with the words in the box.

behind	in	on	under

1. The cell phone is _____ the bag.

2. The bag and the T-shirt are _____ the bed.

3. The T-shirt is _____ the bag.

4. The bag is _____ the girl.

2 Write sentences. Use *there's / there are* (✓) or *there isn't / there aren't* (✗) and the words in parentheses.

1. *(a cell phone / on the table)* ✗

    There isn't a cell phone on the table.

2. *(windows / in the bathroom)* ✓

    _____

3. *(a chair / behind the desk)* ✓

    _____

4. *(a computer / on the table)* ✗

    _____

5. *(any headphones / under the desk)* ✗

    _____

3 Write questions with *Is there* or *Are there* and the words in parentheses. Then look at the picture and write the answers.

1. *(a lamp / on the table?)*

    Is there _____

    _____

2. *(a chair / in the living room?)*

    _____

    _____

3. *(any curtains / on the window?)*

    _____

    _____

4 **Correct the sentences.**

1. ~~There's~~ some books on the desk ✗

   There are some books on the desk.

2. There ~~aren't~~ a TV in the kitchen. ✗

   _____

3. ~~Is~~ a sofa in the living room? ✗

   _____

4. There ~~no is~~ a closet in the bedroom. ✗

   _____

5. There aren't ~~a~~ books in the drawer. ✗

   _____

6. ~~Are~~ any windows in in the kitchen? ✗

   _____

5 **Complete the conversation with the questions in the box.**

| Is there a lamp? | is there a table? | Where's the chair? | ~~Where's the desk?~~ |

Will   This is the bedroom.

Jung-soo   ¹ _Where's the desk?_____

Will   There isn't a desk.

Jung-soo   Oh, ² _____

Will   Of course! There's a table in the kitchen.

Jung-soo   ³ _____

Will   Yes, there is. It's behind the chair.

Jung-soo   ⁴ _____

Will   It's right behind you!

6 **Write questions with _Is there_ or _Are there_ and the words in parentheses.**
Then write true answers about your bedroom.

1. (any curtains / on the windows?)

   _____?

   _____.

2. (a closet / in the bedroom?)

   _____?

   _____.

3. (a TV / in the bedroom?)

   _____?

   _____.

4. (any shoes / under the bed?)

   _____?

   _____.

LISTENING

GO
ONLINE Go to www.smartchoicepractice.com. Download the audio for Unit 8.

🔊 **1** Listen. Which apartment are they in? Choose the correct picture.

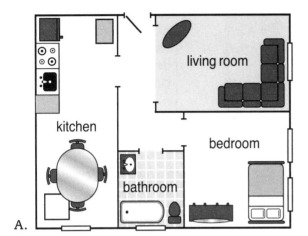

A.

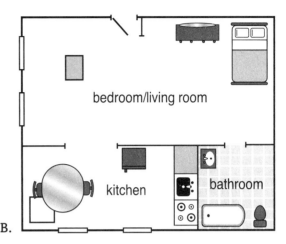

B.

🔊 **2** Listen again. Choose (✓) *True* or *False*.

	True	False
1. Monica and Valerie are talking about their new apartment.	☐	☐
2. There aren't any beds in the apartment.	☐	☐
3. There's a kitchen.	☐	☐
4. There isn't a sofa.	☐	☐
5. There are two broken chairs.	☐	☐
6. There are two TVs.	☐	☐

PRONUNCIATION

🔊 **1** Listen to the sentences. Circle the stressed words.

1. (Welcome) to our new (apartment)!
2. This is the bedroom.
3. Well, it's really the bedroom and the living room.
4. Where are the beds?
5. Well, it's old, but comfortable.
6. Oh, is there a chair?
7. There are two brand-new chairs in the kitchen.
8. And where's the TV?

READING

1 Read the texts quickly. Which bedroom does the picture show?

Text ____

ROOM TO RENT

Large room in an apartment near center of town. There are two beds and two brand-new desks. There's also a large closet and a sofa.

$**700**/month.

Call Julian at
356-7287

A

Apartment

Studio to rent.
In the bedroom / living room, there's a comfortable bed, a sofa, a desk, and a chair.
In the kitchen, there's a table with four chairs.

$**1,000**/month.

Call Kim at
435-7698

B

Bedroom

Nice room in house in center of town. There's a small closet, a brand-new bed, a desk, and two chairs.

$**350** a month.

after 6 p.m.
Monday to
Friday.

Call Mike at
933-7261

C

2 Which ad do these sentences describe: A, B, or C?

1. There are two rooms.   B

2. There isn't a sofa.   ____

3. There are two brand-new desks.   ____

4. There aren't any chairs.   ____

5. There is a small closet.   ____

6. There are five chairs.   ____

9 | The bank is on the corner.

VOCABULARY

1 What places do the signs show? Complete the labels with the place words.

1. p a r k

2. b ___ ___ ___

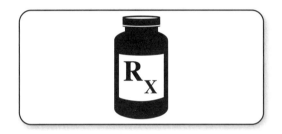

3. d ___ ___ ___ ___ ___ ___ ___ ___ ___

4. p ___ ___ ___   o ___ ___ ___ ___ ___ ___

5. s ___ ___ ___ ___ ___
   s ___ ___ ___ ___ ___ ___

6. p ___ ___ ___ ___ ___
   r ___ ___ ___ ___ ___ ___ ___

2 Write true sentences about places near your school. Use the words in Activity 1.

1. There's a park. / There isn't a park.

2. _____

3. _____

4. _____

5. _____

LANGUAGE PRACTICE

1 Look at the map. Complete the sentences with the words in the box.

across from	between
~~next to~~	on the corner of

1. The drugstore is _next to_ the convenience store.

2. The department store is _____ the subway station.

3. The public restrooms are _____ First Street and East Avenue.

4. The park is _____ the post office and the bank.

2 Look at the map in Activity 1 again. Write questions and answers. Use *where* and the words in parentheses.

1. (*convenience store*)

   Where's the convenience store _____?

   It's _____.

2. (*subway station*)

   _____?

   _____.

3. (*post office*)

   _____?

   _____.

3 Look at the map in Activity 1 again. You are at the *X*. Follow the directions. Where are you now?

1. Go straight on Second Street and cross West and East Avenues. It's next to the convenience store. _drugstore_

2. Go straight on Second Street and turn left on West Avenue. It's across from the department store. _____

3. Go straight on Second Street and turn right on East Avenue. It's on the corner of Second and East, next to the park. _____

50

4 Complete the conversation. Use the words in the box.

across from	go straight	Is there a	on the corner
on the corner of	right on	Straight on	turn right

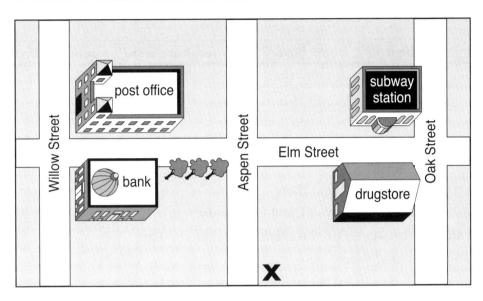

Alex Excuse me. [1] <u>Is there a</u> subway station near here?

Man A subway station? Yes, it's [2] _____ Elm and Oak.

Alex Elm and Oak?

Man Yes, [3] _____ on Aspen Street, and [4] _____ on Elm Street.

Alex [5] _____ Aspen and [6] _____ Elm?

Man That's right. The subway station is [7] _____, [8] _____ the drugstore.

Alex Thanks a lot!

Man You're welcome.

5 Read the conversation in Activity 4 again. Write a similar conversation. Use the map in Activity 4.

Denise Excuse me. [1] <u>Is there a</u> bank [2] _____?

Woman [3] _____? Yes, it's [4] _____ Elm and Willow.

Denise [5] _____ and [6] _____?

Woman Yes, [7] _____ Aspen Street, and turn [8] _____ on Elm Street at the traffic lights.

Denise [9] _____ and [10] _____?

Woman That's right. The bank [11] _____, [12] _____ post office.

Denise Thanks a lot!

Woman [13] _____.

LISTENING

GO
ONLINE Go to www.smartchoicepractice.com. Download the audio for Unit 9.

🔊**1** Listen to the conversations. Where does she want to go? Choose (✓) the box.

	bank	library	furniture store	police station
Conversation 1				
Conversation 2				

🔊**2** Listen again. Choose the correct words.

1. There (is / isn't) a furniture store near there.
2. The furniture store is (next to / across from) the library.
3. The furniture store is (between / on the corner of) Main and Elm.
4. There (is / isn't) a bank near there.
5. The bank is (next to / across from) the police station.
6. The police station is on (Oak Street / Spring Street).

PRONUNCIATION

🔊**1** Listen to the conversations. Mark the intonation above the confirmation questions.

1. A Is there a furniture store near here?

    B A furniture store?

2. A Yes, it's next to the library.

    B Next to the library?

3. A On the corner of Main and Elm.

    B On the corner of Main and Elm?

4. A Is there a bank near here?

    B A bank?

5. A There's one on Spring Street.

    B Spring Street?

6. A The bank's across from the police station.

    B Across from the police station?

READING

1 Read the text. Which places are mentioned?

- ☑ bank
- ☐ convenience store
- ☐ department store
- ☐ gas station
- ☐ traffic lights
- ☐ park
- ☐ post office
- ☐ public restrooms
- ☐ subway station

🔄 ← → 🔍 http://www.reviewahotel.com ☰

Review by Larry, Indiana, March 15
Rate ★★★★

CHECK RATES!

Great location!
The hotel is very small (there are only 20 rooms, only 10 of them with a bathroom), but it's very well located. It's right downtown, so you have all the services you need. There is a large department store on State Avenue (Maximus Department Store) and lots of small stores near it. There is also a convenience store just across from the hotel, on the corner. For those postcards you are sending your family and friends, there is a post office next to the convenience store. And if you need money, there is a bank next to the post office. The subway station is just a few blocks from the hotel, on the corner of State and First. And if you are driving, there's a gas station across from the subway station. And if you just want to relax, go to the park on State Avenue, just across from Maximus. It's beautiful!

---

2 Read the text again. Choose (✓) *True* or *False*. Correct the false sentences.

	True	False
1. There are 10 rooms in the hotel.	☐	☑

There are 20 rooms in the hotel.

	True	False
2. The department store is on First Avenue.	☐	☐

_____

	True	False
3. The hotel is far from downtown.	☐	☐

_____

	True	False
4. The post office is between the convenience store and the bank.	☐	☐

_____

	True	False
5. There is a department store across from the park.	☐	☐

_____

	True	False
6. There is a subway station on the corner of Maximus and First.	☐	☐

_____

	True	False
7. The gas station is across from the hotel.	☐	☐

_____

VOCABULARY

1 Choose the best answers to complete the text.

```
○ ○ ○
To:      sara.smith@yoohoo.com
From:    katie.rogers@webemail.com
Subject: Hello

I'm sending you a photo of me and my
friend in our dorm. I'm wearing ¹_____
and a ²_____. Our room is very nice.
You can't see it, but it's a big room.
There are two beds, a ³_____, and a
⁴_____. There isn't a ⁵_____, but we can
watch movies on the computer. It's not
bad for a dorm room.
```

1. a. skirt
   b. sweater
   c. shirt
   d. jeans

2. a. lamp
   b. shirt
   c. boots
   d. curtains

3. a. windows
   b. park
   c. desk
   d. drugstore

4. a. curtains
   b. windows
   c. chair
   d. bank

5. a. TV
   b. lamp
   c. closet
   d. sofa

2 Choose the best answers to complete the sentences.

1. Alice is ___ casual clothes.
   a. riding
   b. looking
   c. wearing
   d. having

2. James is ___ a soda.
   a. talking
   b. watching
   c. drinking
   d. cooking

3. There's a ___ on the desk.
   a. park
   b. window
   c. library
   d. computer

4. Your T-shirts are ___ the drawer.
   a. on
   b. in
   c. under
   d. behind

5. The convenience store is ___ the corner.
   a. on
   b. next
   c. across
   d. between

6. Is there a public ___ near here?
   a. station
   b. office
   c. restroom
   d. store

7. Thomas plays tennis in the ___.
   a. park
   b. furniture store
   c. subway station
   d. post office

LANGUAGE

1 Choose the best answers to complete the phone conversation.

> **Bob** Hello.
>
> **Mia** Hi, Bob. I can tell you more about the apartment for rent. There aren't many things in it. For example, in the living room, [1]_____ a sofa and [2]_____ two chairs. There's also a brand-new table.
>
> **Bob** That's it? [3]_____ lamps? [4]_____ TV?
>
> **Mia** No, [5]_____ lamps or a TV. But there's a big closet [6]_____ the bedroom …

1. a. are
   b. there are
   c. is
   d. there's

2. a. are
   b. there are
   c. is
   d. there's

3. a. Is there a
   b. Are they
   c. Are there any
   d. Is it

4. a. Is there a
   b. Are they
   c. Are there any
   d. Is it

5. a. there isn't
   b. there isn't a
   c. there aren't any
   d. aren't

6. a. on
   b. between
   c. next
   d. in

2 Choose the best answers to complete the sentences.

1. Jack ___ tennis.
   a. playing
   b. are playing
   c. play
   d. is playing

2. **A** Is she watching TV?
   B Yes, ___.
   a. she does
   b. she is
   c. she watches
   d. she watching

3. I ___ wearing athletic clothes.
   a. 'm not
   b. don't
   c. not am
   d. aren't

4. What ___ doing?
   a. does he
   b. is
   c. he is
   d. is he

5. There's a bank across ___ the police station.
   a. to
   b. next
   c. from
   d. of

6. Turn ___ on First Street.
   a. straight
   b. right
   c. across
   d. cross

CONVERSATION

1 Choose the best sentences to complete the conversations.

1. A _____

   B She's wearing a long red skirt.

   a. What kind of skirt is she wearing?

   b. What does she wear?

   c. What is she doing?

   d. What kind of skirt does she like?

2. A Look at that boy. Isn't he cute?

   B _____

   a. What's cute?

   b. No, he doesn't.

   c. Yes, he does.

   d. Which boy?

3. A Where's the TV?

   B _____

   a. It's right there!

   b. There's a TV.

   c. They're right there!

   d. It's right!

4. A Is there a kitchen?

   B _____

   a. It's in the kitchen.

   b. Nice place!

   c. Welcome!

   d. Of course!

5. A _____

   B They're next to the drugstore.

   a. Where is it?

   b. Excuse me. Where are the
      public restrooms?

   c. Where's the drugstore?

   d. What are the public restrooms?

6. A Where are the traffic lights?

   B _____

   a. They're on the corner of Main
      and First.

   b. It's on the desk.

   c. Yes, there are.

   d. Excuse me.

7. A Thanks a lot!

   B _____

   a. Of course!

   b. That's right!

   c. Excuse me!

   d. You're welcome!

8. A _____

   B Yes, it's across from the park.

   a. Is there a park next to the mall?

   b. Where is the park?

   c. Is there a park near here?

   d. Is there a gas station near here?

9. A Where's the subway station?

   B _____

   a. There's one in the kitchen.

   b. It's under the desk.

   c. It's next to the bank.

   d. Yes. It's across from the park.

10. A _____

    B No, she's talking to her friend.

    a. Is she dancing?

    b. Is he wearing a brown sweater?

    c. Is she at a party?

    d. What's she doing?

11. A Who's that girl?

    B Which girl?

    A _____

    a. Those over there.

    b. Wait.

    c. She's wearing a black dress.

    d. Oh, her?

12. A Go straight on First and turn left
       on West.

    B Straight on First and left on West.

    A _____

    a. Thanks.

    b. That's right.

    c. You're welcome.

    d. Of course.

READING

1 **Read the text and choose the best answers.**

To: Andrew
From: Grace
Subject: Amsterdam

Hi Andrew!

I'm having a great time here in Amsterdam. I'm with my friend Chris. (Do you know Chris? She's in my class at college.) We're at the library right now. Chris is sending an email to her mother, and I'm writing this email to you.

Amsterdam is beautiful. You can rent bikes here and ride around the city. It's a lot of fun. There are lots of great stores and coffee shops. Chris and I go shopping every day! There's a park near the hotel. We play tennis there in the afternoon, and then in the evening we go to the restaurant in the hotel. The food is great. There's also karaoke at the restaurant. Chris likes karaoke, and she sings all her favorite songs. But I don't like karaoke because I can't sing!

Love,

Grace

---

1. Chris is ___.
   a. Grace's brother
   b. Andrew's friend
   c. Grace's sister
   d. Grace's friend

2. At the library, ___.
   a. Chris and Grace are writing emails
   b. Chris and Grace are having coffee
   c. Grace is sending an emails to her parents
   d. Chris is writing an emails to her friend

3. According to Grace's emails, there are lots of great ___.
   a. parks in Amsterdam
   b. karaoke places in Amsterdam
   c. stores in Amsterdam
   d. hotels in Amsterdam

4. Chris and Grace play tennis ___.
   a. in the hotel
   b. in the park
   c. in the furniture store
   d. in the karaoke bar

5. In the evening, they ___.
   a. go to the park
   b. ride bikes around the city
   c. go to a department store
   d. go to the hotel restaurant

6. Grace doesn't like karaoke because ___.
   a. she can't sing
   b. it's so trendy
   c. there isn't a karaoke bar
   d. she doesn't have favorite songs

VOCABULARY

1 Look at the picture. Select (✓) the things you see on the shopping list.

Shopping List

- ✓ rice
- pasta
- bread
- cookies
- cake
- ice cream
- coffee
- tea
- lettuce
- chicken
- fish

2 Match the shopping baskets and the descriptions.

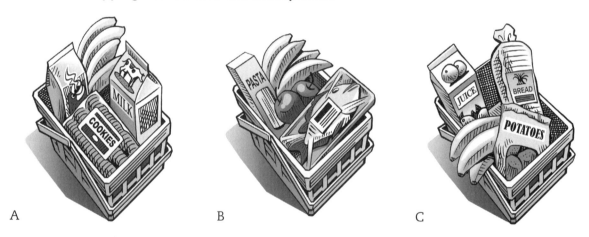

A   B   C

1. There's bread and juice. There are potatoes and bananas. (Basket ___)

2. There's coffee and milk. There are cookies and bananas. (Basket ___)

3. There's pasta and fish. There are apples and bananas. (Basket ___)

LANGUAGE PRACTICE

1 Write *a / an* for count nouns or *some* for noncount nouns.

1. There's _some_ rice.
2. There's _____ pasta.
3. There's _____ potato.
4. There's _____ juice.

5. There's _____ tea.
6. There's _____ tomato.
7. There's _____ lettuce.
8. There's _____ apple.

2 Write sentences. Use *there's* or *there are* and the words in parentheses.

1. (some cookies / on the plate)   _There are some cookies on the plate._

2. (some bread / in the kitchen)   _____

3. (some ice cream / in the freezer)   _____

4. (some bananas / on the table)   _____

5. (some fish / in the refrigerator)   _____

6. (some potatoes / on the stove)   _____

3 Choose *some* or *any*.

1. I need some / any tea. Do we have some / any?
2. We have *some / any* coffee, but we don't have *some / any* milk.
3. There aren't *some / any* tomatoes, but I can buy *some / any*.
4. **A** Are there *some / any* grapes?
   B Yes, there are *some / any* on the table.
5. **A** What do you usually have for lunch?
   B I usually have *some / any* pasta or *some / any* pizza.

4 Complete the conversations. Make A's sentences negative.

1. **A** We need some bread.
   B _We don't need any bread_ . We have some in the kitchen.

2. **A** She wants an apple.
   B _____. She wants a banana.

3. **A** There's some juice in the refrigerator.
   B _____. There's only water.

4. **A** We have some tomatoes.
   B _____. But we have some lettuce.

5 **Correct the sentences.**

1. We don't need ~~some~~ bread. ✗

   <u>We don't need any bread.</u>

2. There's ~~a~~ bread on the table. ✗

   _____

3. There ~~isn't~~ any cookies in the kitchen. ✗

   _____

4. I want ~~some~~ snack. ✗

   _____

5. There ~~are~~ some ice cream in the freezer. ✗

   _____

6. I don't have ~~some~~ juice. ✗

   _____

6 **Complete the conversation. Use *some* and *any*.**

Derek	I'm hungry. Is there ¹ <u>any</u> food?
Holly	There are ² _____ cookies.
Derek	Hmm. What else?
Holly	There's ³ _____ ice cream.
Derek	Is there ⁴ _____ pasta?
Holly	No, there isn't. But I can go shopping.
Derek	Great! Do we have ⁵ _____ chicken?
Holly	No, but I can buy ⁶ _____.
Derek	We don't have ⁷ _____ lettuce, either.
Holly	OK. So pasta, chicken, and lettuce.
Derek	That's right. Thanks!

7 **What food and drinks are there in your kitchen? Write true sentences. Use the words in parentheses.**

1. *(rice)* <u>There's some rice / There isn't any rice.</u>

2. *(coffee)* _____

3. *(fish)* _____

4. *(apples)* _____

5. *(lettuce)* _____

LISTENING

GO
ONLINE Go to www.smartchoicepractice.com. Download the audio for Unit 10.

◀)) **1** Listen to the conversation. Select (✓) six of the foods they talk about.

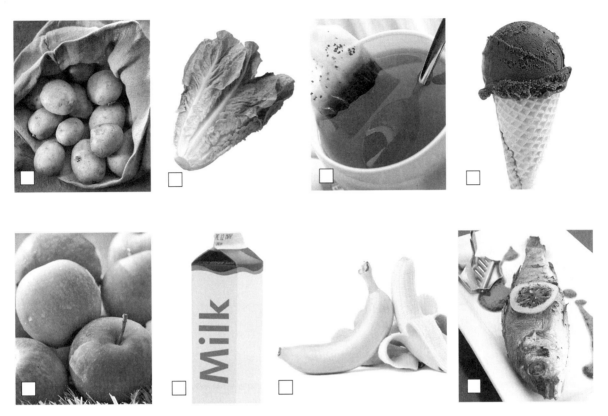

◀)) **2** Listen again. Choose (✓) *True* or *False*.

	True	False
1. They have two slices of pizza.	✓	☐
2. They don't have any bread.	☐	☐
3. They don't have any ice cream.	☐	☐
4. They don't have any cake.	☐	☐
5. They have some large cookies.	☐	☐
6. They don't have any milk.	☐	☐
7. They have some bananas.	☐	☐
8. He's going to the store.	☐	☐

PRONUNCIATION

◀)) **1** Listen to the sentences. Write the intonation above the words in a series.

1. There's some chicken, some lettuce, and some bread.

2. No, but we have some cake, some cookies, and some apples.

3. OK ...So we need ice cream, milk, and bananas.

READING

1 Read the letter. List the food and drink items mentioned.

> Welcome!
>
> The food in the apartment is for you. There are some large apples and bananas on the table in the living room. There's rice, pasta, tea, and coffee in the cabinet in the kitchen. There's water in the refrigerator, but there isn't any juice.
>
> If you need anything, there's a small convenience store on Park Street. Go straight on Main Street and turn left on Park. It's across from the subway station. The convenience store is not cheap, but there aren't any supermarkets near here.
>
> Any problems, call my cell phone: 654-2728.
>
> Enjoy your vacation!
>
> Cassandra

_____apples_____

_____

_____

_____

_____

_____

_____

2 Write questions for these answers. (Sometimes more than one question is possible.)

1. _Are there any apples / bananas_____?

   There are some on the table in the living room.

2. _____?

   Yes, there is. It's in the cabinet in the kitchen.

3. _____?

   Yes, there is. It's in the refrigerator.

4. _____?

   No, there isn't, but there's some water.

5. _____?

   No, there aren't. There's only a convenience store.

6. _____?

   It's on Park Street.

Where were you yesterday?

VOCABULARY

1 Unscramble the letters of the place words.

1. m y g

   gym

2. b a r r l i y

   _____

3. c l o s h o

   _____

4. k r o w

   _____

5. l m a l

   _____

6. d r a m a l u n o t

   _____

7. s m e k u p r e t r a

   _____

8. o m e h

   _____

2 Look at Susan's calendar. Complete the sentences about her week. Use the words in Activity 1.

Monday	Tuesday	Wednesday	Thursday	Friday	Saturday	Sunday

1. On Mondays, Wednesdays, and Fridays, Susan _goes to work, and then she goes to the gym_.

2. On Tuesdays and Thursdays, Susan _____.

3. On Saturdays, Susan _____.

4. On Sundays, Susan _____.

3 Read the sentences about Susan's week in Activity 2 again. Write similar sentences about your week. Use the words in Activity 1 or your own ideas.

1. _On_ _____

2. _____

3. _____

63

LANGUAGE PRACTICE

1 **Complete the sentences. Use *was* or *were*.**

1. Dana __was__ at the park this morning. It __was__ great!

2. Jenny and Emma _____ at the mall yesterday. It _____ OK.

3. I _____ at a rock concert last night. The music _____ awful!

4. Ricky and I _____ at the library on Saturday. It _____ good.

5. Keith _____ at the supermarket last night. It _____ OK.

6. I _____ at a party on Friday. It _____ great!

2 **Complete the text. Use *was*, *were*, *wasn't*, or *weren't*.**

Yesterday ¹ __was__ Sunday, so I ² _____ at work. I was at home. My husband goes to the gym on Sundays, but he wasn't at the gym yesterday. He ³ _____ at home with me. But our children ⁴ _____ there. They were at the park all day with my sister. In the evening, we ⁵ _____ all at a concert. But it ⁶ _____ good. It was awful!

3 **Complete the questions and answers. Use the information in the chart.**

1. __Was__ Bill at the laundromat last Sunday?

   __Yes, he was__ .

2. _____ Bill and Tina at the park last Sunday?

   _____ .

3. _____ Bill at the supermarket last Saturday?

   _____ .

4. _____ Bill and Tina at the mall last Sunday?

   _____ .

5. _____ Tina at the gym last Saturday?

   _____ .

		Saturday
Bill		supermarket gym
		Sunday
		park laundromat
		Saturday
Tina		laundromat mall
		Sunday
		park home

4 Correct the sentences.

1. We ~~was~~ at the mall last night ✗

   We were at the mall last night.

2. Joe ~~were~~ at the gym yesterday. ✗

   _____

3. I ~~no was~~ at the park. ✗

   _____

4. Where ~~you were~~ all day? ✗

   _____

5 Complete the conversation. Use the sentences in the box.

You were busy!	Was it good?
Where were you on Saturday?	~~How was your weekend?~~
Were Adrian and Elaine there?	

Amber   ¹ _How was your weekend?_____

Claudia   It was OK. I was at a party on Friday.

Amber   ² _____

Claudia   Yes, it was great.

Amber   ³ _____

Claudia   Yes, they were.

Amber   ⁴ _____

Claudia   I was at the supermarket, then I was at the

           laundromat, and then I was at the gym.

Amber   ⁵ _____

Claudia   Yes, I was!

6 Complete the questions. Then write true answers about you.

1. _____ you busy on Friday morning?

   _____.

2. How _____ your day yesterday?

   _____.

3. Where _____ your friends on Saturday?

   _____.

LISTENING

GO
ONLINE Go to www.smartchoicepractice.com. Download the audio for Unit 11.

◄))1 **Listen. Where were they yesterday? Write the places in the chart.**

| home | Susan's party | ~~library~~ | gym |

	all day	**last night**
Maria	library	
Jenny		

◄))2 **Listen again. Choose the correct word to complete the sentences.**

1. The library was (OK / good).
2. Susan's party was (great / awful).
3. Matt (was / wasn't) at the party.
4. Jenny's sisters (were / weren't) at home yesterday.
5. Jenny was (bored / tired) last night.
6. Jenny's friends (were / weren't) there.

PRONUNCIATION

◄))1 **Listen to the sentences. Write the missing words.**

1. _How was_____ your day yesterday?
2. _____ good.
3. _____ busy.
4. _____ the party?
5. _____ great!
6. _____ it?
7. _____ awful!

READING

1 **Read the text quickly. Choose the correct sentence.**

  a. Jerry was at the concert, but Lucy wasn't.
  b. Lucy was at the concert, but Jerry wasn't.
  c. Jerry and Lucy were at the concert.

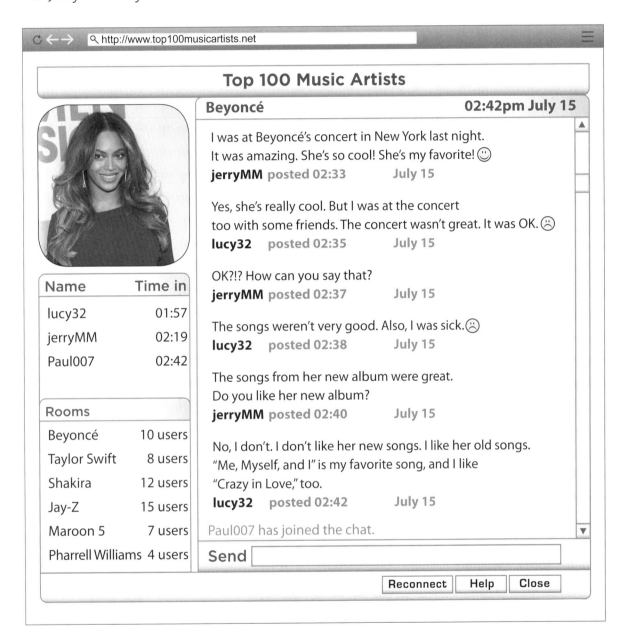

2 **Make true sentences. Complete the sentences with *Jerry*, *Lucy*, or *Jerry and Lucy*.**

  1. <u>Jerry and Lucy</u> were at Beyoncé's concert last night.

  2. Beyoncé is _____'s favorite singer.

  3. _____ was at the concert with some friends.

  4. _____ was sick last night.

  5. _____ likes Beyoncé's new album.

  6. _____ doesn't like Beyoncé's new songs.

VOCABULARY

1 Complete the activities. Use each word in the box only once.

clean	do	go	~~hang out~~	see	stay	take	visit

1. _hang out_ with friends

2. _____ my room

3. _____ a trip

4. _____ home

5. _____ to a party

6. _____ a movie

7. _____ homework

8. _____ family

2 Label the pictures. Use some of the activities from Activity 1.

1. _take a trip_

2. _____

3. _____

4. _____

5. _____

6. _____

3 What do you like to do on weekends? Complete the sentence. Use the activities from Activity 1 or your own ideas.

On weekends, I often _____ or _____, I sometimes
_____, and I never _____.

LANGUAGE PRACTICE

1 Complete the email. Use the simple past.

To: Linda
From: Kelly
Subject: Weekend

Hi, Linda!

How are you? Ralph and I [1] _had_ (have) a great weekend. On Friday evening, we [2] _____ (go) to a great party at Maria's house. Saturday was really nice, so we [3] _____ (play) tennis in the park. In the evening, we [4] _____ (hang out) at a club called Tropicana. We [5] _____ (not go) out on Sunday. We [6] _____ (stay) home. In the afternoon, Ralph [7] _____ (watch) a movie on TV. I [8] _____ (not watch) the movie with him because I rarely watch TV. I [9] _____ (read) a book instead.

How was your weekend?

Kelly

2 Write questions about Kelly and Ralph's weekend. Use the words in parentheses and the simple past of the verbs. Then read the email again and answer the questions.

1. (Kelly and Ralph / have / a great weekend)
   Did Kelly and Ralph have a great
   weekend? Yes, they did.

2. (what / they / do / on Friday night)
   _____?
   _____.

3. (when / they / play / tennis)
   _____?
   _____.

4. (where / they / hang out / on Saturday evening)
   _____?
   _____.

5. (Kelly / go out / on Sunday)
   _____?
   _____.

6. (what / Ralph do / on Sunday afternoon)
   _____?
   _____.

3 Correct the sentences.

1. I ~~goed~~ to a party this weekend. ✗
   I went to a party this weekend.

2. What ~~do you did~~ this weekend? ✗
   _____

3. We didn't ~~visited~~ family on Saturday. ✗
   _____

4. Did you ~~took~~ a trip? ✗
   _____

69

4 **Complete the conversation. Use the questions in the box.**

Did you go shopping?	~~Did you have a good weekend?~~
How was it?	What did you do, then?
What did you do?	Where did you go?

Alison Hi, Simon. [1] _Did you have a good weekend?_

Simon Yes, I did.

Alison [2] _____

Simon I took a trip.

Alison [3] _____

Simon I went to Chicago.

Alison Nice place. [4] _____

Simon No, I didn't. I rarely go shopping.

Alison Oh! [5] _____

Simon I went to a rock concert.

Alison [6] _____

Simon It was great.

5 **Read the conversation in Activity 4 again. Write a similar conversation. Use the information below.**

> Daniel took a trip. He went to New York City. He didn't go to Central Park because he rarely goes to parks. He went to a big department store. It was great.

Lydia Hi, Daniel. [1] _Did you have a good weekend?_

Daniel Yes, [2] _____ .

Lydia [3] _____ ?

Daniel [4] _____ trip.

Lydia [5] _____ ?

Daniel [6] _____ New York City.

Lydia Nice place. [7] _____ Central Park?

Daniel No, [8] _____ . [9] _____ .

Lydia Oh! [10] _____ , then?

Daniel [11] _____ .

Lydia [12] _____ ?

Daniel It was great!

LISTENING

GO
ONLINE Go to www.smartchoicepractice.com. Download the audio for Unit 12.

1 Listen. What did they do last weekend? Match the names and the pictures.

1. Gabriela

2. Leah

A.

B.

2 Listen again. Choose the best answer to complete each sentence.

1. Gabriela's weekend was ___.
   a. not bad
   b. pretty good
   d. great

2. Leah ___ on Friday night.
   a. did homework
   b. hung out with friends
   c. took a trip

3. Leah cleaned her room on ___.
   a. Friday
   b. Saturday
   c. Sunday

4. Leah didn't ___.
   a. visit family
   b. stay home
   c. do homework

5. Gabriela went to ___.
   a. Auckland
   b. Toronto
   c. Seattle

6. The museum was ___.
   a. not interesting
   b. sad
   c. crowded

PRONUNCIATION

1 Listen to the questions. Write the missing words.

1. _Did you_____ have a good weekend?

2. So _____ do?

3. _____ do on Sunday?

4. _____ do this weekend?

5. _____ go?

6. _____ do?

7. _____ fun?

READING

1 **Read the postcard. Answer the questions.**

1. Who is the postcard from? _____

2. Where is she on vacation? _____

3. Who is the postcard to? _____

Dear Barbara,

Jim and I are having a great week in New York City. The weather is fantastic!

On Monday, I went shopping on Fifth Avenue in the morning. In the afternoon, Jim and I went to a concert. On Tuesday, we visited a museum. On Wednesday, we took a trip to Ellis Island and saw the Statue of Liberty. It was interesting. On Thursday, we ate sushi at a great restaurant and then went to a party at a noisy club. Today's Friday, and Jim went to another museum. I stayed at the hotel because I wanted to write postcards.

See you next weekend.

Love

Leah

PLACE
STAMP
HERE

Barbara Knight

526 East St.

Los Angeles

2 **Read the text again. Answer the questions.**

1. Where did Leah and Jim go on Monday afternoon? _They went to a concert._

2. Did Jim go to a museum on Tuesday? _____

3. When did Leah and Jim see the Statue of Liberty? _____

4. What did Leah do on Monday morning? _____

5. What did Leah and Jim eat on Thursday? _____

6. Did Jim stay at the hotel on Friday? _____

VOCABULARY

1 Choose the best answers to complete the text.

> ### Did you have a *busy* weekend?
> ─────────We asked **Josie DeFranco**.
>
> I'm a teacher at a large ¹____, and last week was very busy. I didn't want a busy weekend, too. So, on Saturday morning, I did yoga at the ²____. In the afternoon, I went shopping at a ³____. In the evening, I ⁴____ with friends. On Sunday, I ⁵____ home all day, but I ⁶____ a movie in the evening. Well, I think it was a busy weekend …but it was a lot of fun, too.

1. a. laundromat
   b. supermarket
   c. school
   d. mall

2. a. home
   b. library
   c. supermarket
   d. gym

3. a. department store
   b. library
   c. laundromat
   d. park

4. a. went
   b. took
   c. hung out
   d. saw

5. a. visited
   b. stayed
   c. did
   d. saw

6. a. visited
   b. went
   c. took
   d. saw

2 Choose the best answers to complete the sentences.

1. There isn't any ____ in the refrigerator.
   a. cookies
   b. bananas
   c. apple
   d. milk

2. Do you want a ____?
   a. bread
   b. cookie
   c. ice cream
   d. potatoes

3. There's some ____ in the kitchen.
   a. coffee
   b. apples
   c. potatoes
   d. banana

4. There were a lot of people at the concert. It was ____.
   a. sick
   b. sad
   c. bored
   d. crowded

5. Do you want to take a ____ on Sunday?
   a. movie
   b. trip
   c. party
   d. homework

6. We don't have any bananas. Can you go to the ____?
   a. library
   b. school
   c. laundromat
   d. supermarket

LANGUAGE

1 **Choose the best answers to complete the text.**

> Good morning, Audrey!
>
> Can you go to the supermarket today? We don't have [1]___ milk. We need [2]___ bananas, too. And do we have [3]___ apples for the cake? Maybe you can buy [4]___, too.
>
> By the way, Fran [5]___ here last night. Where [6]___ you?
>
> Chelsea

1. a. some
   b. any
   c. a
   d. an

2. a. some
   b. any
   c. a
   d. an

3. a. some
   b. any
   c. a
   d. an

4. a. some
   b. any
   c. a
   d. an

5. a. was
   b. did
   c. is
   d. went

6. a. were
   b. did
   c. are
   d. go

2 **Choose the best answers to complete the sentences.**

1. Please buy some juice.
   We don't have ___.
   a. a
   b. some
   c. any
   d. no

2. We ___ at school on Friday.
   a. didn't
   b. weren't
   c. wasn't
   d. didn't be

3. They ___ their room this morning.
   a. cleaned
   b. clean
   c. cleans
   d. were

4. ___ he at the gym last night?
   a. Was
   b. Did
   c. Is
   d. Does

5. ___ a trip last week?
   a. Did you
   b. You take
   c. Did you take
   d. Did you took

6. I ___ a movie last weekend.
   a. didn't
   b. don't saw
   c. didn't see
   d. didn't saw

CONVERSATION

1 Choose the best sentence to complete the conversations.

1. A _____

   B Yes. It's on the table.

   a. Do we have any cookies?
   b. Do we have two slices of pizza?
   c. Do we have any juice?
   d. Where's the bread?

2. A Where's the coffee?

   B _____

   a. They're in the fridge.
   b. Yes, we do. It's in the living room.
   c. We don't have any.
   d. No, we don't.

3. A We need some juice and some apples.

   B _____

   a. We don't have any juice.
   b. OK. What else?
   c. It's in the fridge.
   d. I can't.

4. A Do you want to go shopping?

   B _____

   a. I can buy some.
   b. Yes, I can.
   c. We don't have any bananas, either.
   d. I can't. I'm busy.

5. A This kitchen is messy! It's your job to clean it.

   B _____

   a. I was bored.
   b. No, I wasn't!
   c. Well, I was just there.
   d. Sorry! I was too busy.

6. A I wasn't at home this morning.

   B _____

   a. No, I wasn't.
   b. Where were you?
   c. I was at home, too.
   d. Were you at home?

7. A Were you at school all day?

   B _____

   a. Yes, I was.
   b. Sorry, Mom.
   c. No, you weren't.
   d. You were at home.

8. A Where were you this morning?

   B _____

   a. No, I wasn't.
   b. Sorry!
   c. We were at the gym.
   d. You weren't at home.

9. A _____

   B Yeah, it was OK.

   a. What did you do this weekend?
   b. Where did you go?
   c. Did you have a good weekend?
   d. When did you do your homework?

10. A What did you do on Friday evening?

    B _____

    a. They saw a movie.
    b. Yes, I did.
    c. It was noisy!
    d. We went to a party.

11. A When did you visit family?

    B _____

    a. On Sunday.
    b. Yes, I did.
    c. At home.
    d. I was so busy!

12. A _____

    B Yes, we did.

    a. Did he hang out with friends?
    b. Where did you go on Saturday?
    c. When did you clean your room?
    d. Did you take a trip?

READING

1 Read the text and choose the best answers.

> conversation started on Aug 1
>
> **Megan Scott**
>
> Hi, Jordan. How are you? I'm having a great time at college. I'm living in a house with four other students. We have a lot of fun! The house is big—there are five bedrooms, two bathrooms, a kitchen, and a living room. The kitchen is always messy. In fact, I'm in the kitchen now, and there's some milk on the chairs!
>
> I'm busy every day. We have classes from Monday to Friday, and we have a lot of homework. On Saturdays, I go shopping or hang out with friends. On Sundays, I don't usually go out. I clean my room, read, watch TV, or write to my family and friends. But last weekend, the weather was great, so we went to the park!
>
> Yesterday, my friends went shopping at the mall. I was sick, so I didn't go. I stayed home and slept all day. For dinner, I got pizza. I had three large slices of pizza, a small salad, and some orange juice. Then I watched a sad movie on TV. I went to bed early. I feel better today. Speak soon!

1. Megan is a ___ .
   a. teacher
   b. student
   c. waiter
   d. doctor

2. Megan lives in ___ .
   a. a big house
   b. a small house
   c. an apartment
   d. a park

3. Megan goes to school ___ .
   a. every day
   b. on Saturdays
   c. on Sundays
   d. from Monday to Friday

4. Megan goes shopping ___ .
   a. every day
   b. on Saturdays
   c. on Sundays
   d. on Fridays

5. Last weekend, Megan ___ .
   a. went to the mall
   b. played video games
   c. went to the park
   d. stayed home

6. Megan was ___ yesterday.
   a. shopping
   b. sick
   c. bored
   d. sad

AUDIO SCRIPTS

LISTENING .... p. 4

1. **Sara** Hi. I'm Sara Johnson.
    Bill Hi, Sara. I'm Bill Brown. Nice to meet you.
    S Nice to meet you, too. Are you a server here?
    B No, I'm not. I'm a chef. How about you?
    S I'm a server.
    B Are you from New York, Sara?
    S Yes, I am. How about you?
    B No, I'm from Miami.

2. **Katie** Hi. My name is Katie.
    Jonah Hello, Katie. Nice to meet you. I'm Jonah Ward.
    K Are you an artist here, Jonah?
    J No, I'm an actor. How about you?
    K I'm a model.
    J Are you from Los Angeles, Katie?
    K Yes, I am. How about you?
    J No, I'm not from Los Angeles. I'm from Detroit.

PRONUNCIATION .... p. 4

1. S Are you a server here?
2. B I'm a chef.
3. S I'm a server.
4. S Are you an artist here?
5. B No, I'm an actor.
6. S I'm a model.

LISTENING .... p. 9

1. **Senji** Hey, Pedro!
    Pedro Hi, Senji. What's your email address?
    S My email address? Why?
    P For the tennis club directory.
    S It's Senji. That's S-E-N-J-I – dash Tanaka at go dot net. Tanaka is T-A-N-A-K-A.
    P Great! And what's your phone number?
    S My phone number is 535-555-7274.
    P OK. That's 535-555-7247…
    S No, it's 535-555-7274.
    P OK. Thank you, Senji.
    S You're welcome.

2. **Pedro** Violeta, what's your email address?
    Violeta It's V underscore A-H-N at yoohoo dot com.
    P Great! And what's your phone number?
    V My phone number is 371-555-0231.
    P Thanks, Violeta.
    V You're welcome.

3. **Pedro** And, Jane, how about Ana Morales? She isn't here now. What's her phone number?
    Jane It's 24-4355-0629.
    P Is that 24-435-0629?
    J No, 24-4355-0629. She's in Brazil now.
    P Oh! Well, what's her email?
    J It's ana dot morales – that's A-N-A dot M-O-R-A-L-E-S – at go dot net.
    P OK, great! Thanks!
    J You're welcome.

PRONUNCIATION .... p. 9

1. S My phone number is 535-555-7274.
2. P OK. That's 535-555-7247.
3. V My phone number is 371-555-0231.
4. J It's 24-4355-0629.
5. P Is that 24-435-0629?

LISTENING .... p. 14

1. A Hey, Pete! Is that your white dog?
    Pete No, it isn't. It's my brother's dog.
    A What's the dog's name?
    P It's Skippy!
    A How old is he?
    P He's 13 years old.
    A Wow! That's old!

2. A Hey, Sam. What's your phone number?
    Sam It's 209-7312.
    A And what's your address?
    S My address is 80 Oak Street.
    A What's your email address?
    S It's Sam16 at yoohoo dot com.

3. A Are these your pictures, Linda?
    Linda Yes, they are!
    A Who are those people?
    L They're my grandparents!
    A How old are they?
    L Let's see… my grandmother is 70 and my grandfather is 82.
    A Wow! They're old!

4. A Who are those girls in the red car?
    B Those are my friends, Kim and Tara.
    A Are they sisters?
    B Yes, they are!
    A How old are they?
    B Kim is 14 and Tara is 19.

PRONUNCIATION . . . . p. 14

1. **P** He's 13 years old.
    A Wow! That's old!
2. **A** And what's your address?
    S My address is 80 Oak Street.
3. **A** What's your email address?
    S It's Sam16 at yoohoo dot com.
4. **A** How old are they?
    L Let's see… my grandmother is 70 and my grandfather is 82.
5. **A** How old are they?
    B Kim is 14 and Tara is 19.

LISTENING . . . . p. 23

Alice Hey, Tom, is this your music?
Tom No, it isn't, Alice. It's my brother's.
A Does your brother like hip-hop?
T Yes, he does. He loves it.
A Wow! Is this the new Jay-Z song?
T Yes, it is. Do you like hip-hop?
A Yes, I do. I think it's catchy. How about you?
T No, I'm sorry. I think hip-hop is boring.
A Do you like rock music?
T Yes, rock music is OK. But my favorite kind of music is jazz. I love the trumpet.
A I like jazz, too. Does your brother like jazz?
T Yes, he does. Let's listen to some jazz.
A Great idea!

PRONUNCIATION . . . . p. 23

1. **A** Is this your music?
2. **A** Does your brother like hip-hop?
3. **A** Is this the new Jay-Z song?
4. **T** Do you like hip-hop?
5. **A** Do you like rock music?
6. **A** Does your brother like jazz?

LISTENING . . . . p. 28

Mike Hi, Tara!
Tara Hey, Mike! Do you do yoga?
M No, I don't. How about you? Do you do yoga?
T Yes, I do.
M Where do you do yoga?
T I do yoga at school.

M Really? That's great!
T So what do you do for fun? Do you play video games?
M Yes, I do! I really like video games. I also love shopping online. How about you? Do you like video games?
T Yes, I do, too!
M What's your favorite game?
T My favorite game is Fire Ring!
M That game is amazing!
T Let's play video games together! Are you free on Thursday?
M Thursday? No, I'm not.
T Well, when are you free?
M I'm free on Friday after school!
T Great! Let's play video games on Friday! Send me a text message after school.
M OK, great!

PRONUNCIATION . . . . p. 28

1. **T** Do you do yoga?
2. **M** Where do you do yoga?
3. **T** So what do you do for fun?
4. **T** Do you play video games?
5. **M** Do you like video games?
6. **M** What's your favorite game?
7. **T** Are you free on Thursday?
8. **T** Well, when are you free?

LISTENING . . . . p. 33

Terry So, Brett, do you like music?
Brett Yes, Terry, I do! I love music!
T Great! What can you do?
B Well, let's see… I can't play the guitar and I can't play the piano.
T Hmm…. Can you sing?
B No, I can't. I can't sing at all! I only sing at home!
T So, what can you do, then?
B I can dance! How about you, Terry? Can you dance?
T No, I can't! But I can play the piano and I can play the guitar! I play in a band at school.
B That's great! And can you sing?
T Yes, I can. I can sing very well.

PRONUNCIATION . . . . p. 33

1. **T** What can you do?
2. **B** I can't play the guitar.

3. **B** I can't play the piano.

4. **T** Can you sing?

5. **B** I can't sing at all!

6. **B** I can dance!

7. **T** But I can play the piano.

8. **T** I can play the guitar.

UNIT 7

LISTENING . . . . p. 42

Andrew   Hello?

Daria   Hi, Andrew! It's Daria!

A Oh, hi, Daria! Are you at the gym?

D No, I'm not. I'm at school.

A What are you doing?

D I'm doing my homework and talking to you!

A Is Maria there?

D Yes, she is. What's she doing?

A She's listening to music and sending text messages.

D What kind of music is she listening to?

A Hip-hop.

D Cool! How about Tony? Is he there?

A No, he's wearing athletic clothes today, so I think he's at the gym. So, where are you?

D I'm at home. I'm shopping online.

A What are you buying?

D Business clothes for my new job… uh, time to go! My mom's calling me!

A OK, bye!

D Talk to you later!

PRONUNCIATION . . . . p. 42

1. **D** What are you doing?

2. **A** What kind of music is she listening to?

3. **A** What's she doing?

4. **D** What are you buying?

UNIT 8

LISTENING . . . . p. 47

Valerie   Hi, Monica! Welcome to our new apartment! Come on in!

Monica   Thanks, Valerie. Hmm… this is an interesting place.

V This is the bedroom. Well, it's really the bedroom and the living room.

M Where are the beds?

V They're right behind you. That's your bed.

M It looks old.

V Well, it's old, but comfortable.

M OK, that's good. And, where's the sofa?

V There isn't a sofa.

M Oh, is there a chair?

V Of course! There are two brand-new chairs in the kitchen.

M And where's the TV?

V It's right here!

PRONUNCIATION . . . . p. 47

1. **V** Welcome to our new apartment!

2. **V** This is the bedroom.

3. **V** Well, it's really the bedroom and the living room.

4. **M** Where are the beds?

5. **V** Well, it's old, but comfortable.

6. **M** Oh, is there a chair?

7. **V** There are two brand-new chairs in the kitchen.

8. **M** And where's the TV?

UNIT 9

LISTENING . . . . p. 52

1. **A** Excuse me! Is there a furniture store near here?

   B A furniture store? Yes, it's next to the library.

   A Next to the library?

   B Yes, it's on Elm Street… On the corner of Main and Elm.

   A On the corner of Main and Elm? Great! Thanks!

   B You're welcome!

2. **A** Excuse me! Is there a bank near here?

   B A bank? Yes, there's one on Spring Street.

   A Spring Street?

   B Yes. Cross Oak Street and turn right on Spring at the traffic lights. The bank's across from the police station.

   A Across from the police station?

   B That's right.

   A Thanks a lot!

   B You're welcome!

PRONUNCIATION . . . . p. 52

1. **A** Is there a furniture store near here?

   B A furniture store?

2. **A** Yes, it's next to the library.

   B Next to the library?

3. **B** On the corner of Main and Elm.

   A On the corner of Main and Elm?

4. **A** Is there a bank near here?

   B A bank?

5. **B** There's one on Spring Street.

   A Spring Street?

6. **B** The bank's across from the police station.
    A Across from the police station?

LISTENING .... p. 61

A Hey, Dad, I'm hungry. Is there any food in the house?
Dad Let's see... there are some potatoes and two slices of pizza.
A What else?
D There's some chicken, some lettuce, and some bread. Do you want a chicken sandwich?
A Hmm... no, not really... Do we have any ice cream?
D No, but we have some cake, some cookies, and some apples.
A Are they the large cookies?
D No, they are small.
A Is there any milk?
D No, there isn't. But I can go shopping.
A Great! Do we have any bananas?
D No, but I can buy some.
A Thank you!
D OK... So we need ice cream, milk, and bananas.
A Great. I can have some ice cream with a banana and some milk.

PRONUNCIATION .... p. 61

1. **D** There's some chicken, some lettuce, and some bread.
2. **D** No, but we have some cake, some cookies, and some apples.
3. **D** So we need ice cream, milk, and bananas.

LISTENING .... p. 66

Jenny Hi, Maria! How was your day yesterday?
Maria Hey, Jenny! It was good. I was at the library all day.
J How was it?
M It was busy. There were a lot of people there.
J Were you there at the library last night, too?
M No, I was at Susan's party.
J How was the party?
M It was great!
J Really? Was Matt there?
M Yes, he was. How about you? How was your day yesterday?
J It was OK. I was at home all day. My sisters were there, too.

M Where were you last night?
J I was at the gym.
M How was it?
J It was awful! My friends weren't there, so I was bored.
M Really? That's too bad!

PRONUNCIATION .... p. 66

1. **J** How was your day yesterday?
2. **M** It was good.
3. **M** It was busy.
4. **J** How was the party?
5. **M** It was great!
6. **M** How was it?
7. **J** It was awful!

LISTENING .... p. 71

Gabriela Hey, Leah!
Leah Hi, Gabriela! Did you have a good weekend?
G Yes! It was pretty good! How about you? Did you have a good weekend?
L Yeah... my weekend wasn't bad.
G So what did you do?
L Well, I hung out with friends on Friday night, and on Saturday I stayed home and did homework.
G What did you do on Sunday?
L Oh, nothing interesting. I stayed home and cleaned my room. How about you? What did you do this weekend?
G I took a trip!
L Where did you go?
G I went to visit family in Toronto.
L Really? What did you do?
G We went to a museum.
L Did you have fun?
G Yes, I did! It was crowded, but interesting.
L That's great!

PRONUNCIATION .... p. 71

1. **L** Did you have a good weekend?
2. **G** So what did you do?
3. **G** What did you do on Sunday?
4. **L** What did you do this weekend?
5. **L** Where did you go?
6. **L** What did you do?
7. **L** Did you have fun?

198 Madison Avenue
New York, NY 10016 USA

Great Clarendon Street, Oxford, OX2 6DP, United Kingdom

Oxford University Press is a department of the University of Oxford.
It furthers the University's objective of excellence in research, scholarship,
and education by publishing worldwide. Oxford is a registered trade
mark of Oxford University Press in the UK and in certain other countries

ISBN: 978 0 19 460251 8 (WORKBOOK)

Printed in China

This book is printed on paper from certified and well-managed sources

ACKNOWLEDGMENTS

*Illustrations by: Kevin Brown pp.30, 33, 44, 58, 71; Scott MacNeill pp.6, 39, 47, 50, 51,
63; Marc Mones: pp. 4, 9, 12, 20, 68; Gavin Reece pp.22, 40, 45, 46; William Waitzman
pp. 1, 13, 14, 23, 25, 45.*

*The publishers would like to thank the following for permission to reproduce photographs:
Cover: Martin Barraud/Getty Images; Mint Images/Tim Pannell/Getty Images; 4x6/
iStockphoto. p.2 Christy Thompson/Shutterstock, Gina Smith/Shutterstock, Rubberball/
Punchstock, Andriy Bezuglov/Alamy Stock Photo; p.3 PhotoAlto / Alamy Stock Photo;
p.5 Fancy/OUP, wavebreakmedia/Shutterstock, wizdata/Shutterstock, Tim Hall/Getty
Images; p.6 michaeljung/Shutterstock; p.7 Image Source/OUP, PT Images/Shutterstock,
yitewang/OUP, Businessvector/OUP, JStone/Shutterstock; p.8 Wavebreak Media ltd/Alamy
Stock Photo; p.11 grocap/Shutterstock, Rafa Irusta/Shutterstock, Bornfree/Shutterstock,
Mega Pixel/Shutterstock, www.BillionPhotos.com/Shutterstock, Epsicons/Shutterstock,
Hysteria/Shutterstock, Alexander Demyanenko/OUP, Robyn Mackenzie/Shutterstock;
p.15 tale/Shutterstock; p.17 Image Source/Punchstock; p.19 GoGo Images Corporation/
Alamy Stock Photo; p.21 Blend Images/OUP; p.24 Paul Bradbury/Getty Images; p.27
Comstock/Punchstock; p.29 S.Borisov/Shutterstock; p.31 White/OUP, Radius Images/
OUP; p.32 Robert Crum/Shutterstock; p.34 BrianBrew/iStock.com; p.36 Norman Pogson/
Shutterstock; p.38 StockLite/Shutterstock, Shelly Perry/iStock.com, billnoll/iStock.com;
p.41 Comstock Images/Getty Images; p.43 Image Source/Alamy Stock Photo, Antonio
Guillem/Shutterstock; p.48 Built Images/Punchstock; p.53 Steve Hamblin/OUP; p.54
Adam Hester/Getty Images; p.57 Photodisc/OUP; p.60 Radius Images/Punchstock; p.61
Crisp/Shutterstock, Danny Smythe/Shutterstock, gennady/Shutterstock, Elena Elisseeva/
Shutterstock, Elena Leonova/Shutterstock, HomeStudio/Shutterstock, Alenavlad/
Shutterstock, Shebeko/Shutterstock; p.64 Yuri Arcurs/Shutterstock; p.65 Monkey Business
Images/Shutterstock; p.67 Monica Schipper/Getty Images; p.70 Yuri Arcurs/Shutterstock;
p.72 Digital Vision/OUP; p.76 krivenko/Shutterstock. Back Cover: martellostudio/
iStockphoto; stockshoppe/Shutterstock.*